KV-618-096

John Boorman was born in London in 1933. His career as a film director includes *Point Blank*, *Deliverance*, *Excalibur* and *Hope and Glory*. He is a five-time Academy Award nominee and was twice awarded Best Director at the Cannes Film Festival. He is the author of a memoir, *Adventures of a Suburban Boy*, as well as *Money Into Light: The Emerald Forest Diary*, and is also the co-founder and editor of Faber's long-running series *Projections: Film-makers on Film-making*.

Further praise for *Conclusions*:

'He has roamed almost every landscape in genre and art cinema – from action-adventure to autobiography – while staying in step with a style you could broadly call "intimate-mythic" . . . There *is* something special about Boorman. It suffuses his delightful, wry, human and elegiacally thoughtful book . . . This man is a very good writer.' Nigel Andrews, *Financial Times*

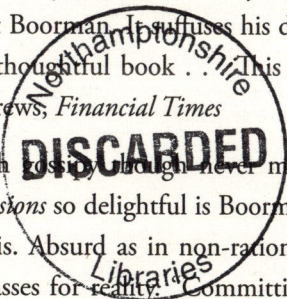
Northamptonshire Libraries DISCARDED

'The chapters teem with gossipy though never mean anecdotes . . . What makes *Conclusions* so delightful is Boorman's awareness of how absurd cinema is. Absurd as in non-rational, dreamlike, an escape from what passes for reality. "Committing yourself to the life of a film-maker is to embrace a form of joyous slavery," he writes. What romance!' Sukhdev Sandhu, *Guardian*

'Boorman may be the most inspired and wayward of English directors since Michael Powell . . . If you live in the darkness of the cinema and are uneasy with other lights, the conclusion of *Conclusions* may surprise you and expose you to your limits.' David

2/22

8000375091

'Boorman has loved the cinema with a passion.'
Roger Lewis, *Daily Telegraph*

'You get a more detailed sense of his spiritual adventures in a delightful new volume titled *Conclusions* . . . *Conclusions* is not a formal autobiography, but the skeleton of the life is all there . . . The opening chapter sketches boarding-house scenes that might delight connoisseurs of the form, such as Patrick Hamilton . . . One notable aspect of the book is its lack of spite and lack of regret.'
Donald Clarke, *Irish Times*

JOHN
BOORMAN

Conclusions

faber

First published in the UK and the USA in 2020
by Faber & Faber Ltd
Bloomsbury House
74–77 Great Russell Street
London WC1B 3DA
This paperback edition first published in 2022

Typeset by Faber & Faber Ltd
Printed and bound in the UK by CPI Group (UK) Ltd, Croydon CR0 4YY

All rights reserved
© John Boorman, 2020
Illustrations © Susan Morley, 2020

'Kingdoms' by John Montague is reproduced
by kind permission of Elizabeth Montague

The right of John Boorman to be identified as author
of this work has been asserted in accordance with Section 77
of the Copyright, Designs and Patents Act 1988

*This book is sold subject to the condition that it shall not, by way of trade or otherwise, be
lent, resold, hired out or otherwise circulated without the publisher's prior consent in any
form of binding or cover other than that in which it is published and without a similar
condition including this condition being imposed on the subsequent purchaser*

A CIP record for this book
is available from the British Library

ISBN 978–0–571–35380–4

FSC
MIX
Paper from
responsible sources
FSC® C171272
www.fsc.org

WEST NORTHAMPTONSHIRE COUNCIL	
80003755091	
Askews & Holts	
CO	

10 9 8 7 6 5 4 3 2 1

For Hope

PREFACE

In old age, words escape me. If I wait patiently, they float up, and I recapture them. If that fails, I am obliged to go down to the cellar, where they languish, and drag them back up. I note that water is starting to seep into the cellar. I fear some words will drown and be lost for ever. The quest for harmony of word and image has been my life. Sight loss is making the world look like late Turners. While I still can, I hasten to testify.

TYPEWRITER

When I left school at sixteen, my teacher and mentor, Fr John Maguire, encouraged me to believe I could be a writer. He told my mother. Coming from modest beginnings, such overweening ambition did not sit well with my painful shyness. It was 1949.

My mother paid two shillings a week into an endowment policy, handing the money to a man who called every week to collect it. She cashed the policy in and bought me a second-hand portable typewriter, my entire inheritance. I got a job collecting and delivering dry cleaning house to house and rented a bedsit on Richmond Hill, where I sat every night tapping away with two fingers, a bottle of Tipp-Ex at hand.

My landlady was a gangling, distraught woman who had inherited several rundown houses that she let out to people like me. My gas meter took penny pieces. These large, antiquated coins (some still with Queen Victoria's head embossed on them) would quickly fill the meter up, until it would take no more. My gas fire would expire, and I would have to ask my landlady, who lived next door, to come and empty the meter. Often she had taken to her bed; if not, she would invite me in for a drink and then complain that she was too wobbly to come and do it. One evening her phone rang. It was the fire brigade to tell her that one of her houses was burning down. 'Thank God for that,' she cried.

I acquired a pair of gloves, cut off the two typing fingers and tapped out my stories in an overcoat. Eventually, my landlady tired of emptying my choked meter and removed the coin reservoir. Thereafter, I used the same penny over and over, making a tick on the wall each time it went through.

A further distraction was a beautiful older woman who lived upstairs. I listened for the front door opening and would dash out into the hallway to catch a glimpse of her. Once I contrived to brush past her and a hint of her lily of the valley clung to me. I went back inside, took off my jacket, buried my face in it and inhaled her perfume. I was so in love it was impossible to banish her from my thoughts, and my writing suffered. I never found the courage to speak to her, but one day she knocked on my door. She had come to seduce me. No, she wanted to borrow pennies for her meter. I gave her my only penny. She smiled at my lovesick face and asked me how old I was. 'Nearly seventeen,' I said. 'And you, how old are you?'

'Nineteen.' Bedsit dreamers awaiting the call.

My friend David was a year older than I and was called up for two years of National Service, as I would be a year or so later. To my great envy he had just landed a job as a clapper-loader at Shepperton Film Studios, which he would lose if he had to go into the army for two years, so he registered as a conscientious objector. He was called before a tribunal to test his sincerity. He failed to convince his examiners and was ordered to enlist. He refused and was jailed for three months. The way it worked was that if you were prepared to go to prison, it proved you were sincere, and therefore should not have gone to prison.

I went to visit David in Wormwood Scrubs. I took my place opposite him in a line of sobbing wives and broken-hearted mothers. David regaled me with stories of his incarceration. There was a tame sparrow they fed crumbs to. Three old lags had brutal fights to decide whose it was. Some of the women visitors complained to the guard about our hilarity and I was thrown out, ejected from prison for laughing.

I wrote the story up, but no magazine would take it. However, several of my pieces did get published. One was about the limbo of waiting for the call-up to the military.

At the time, BBC radio was putting out some youth programmes. The producer read my piece and invited me to take part. It was helpful. I was paid five guineas for each broadcast, and there was my name in the *Radio Times*. I was supporting myself with my typewriter. I could give up the day job.

I put forward ideas. I proposed that I should visit all the film studios and interview the technicians about their jobs. I was besotted with the movies and wanted to find out how they were done. I did the lighting gaffer and his best boy, the focus-puller, the continuity girl, the clapper-loader, the standby props man. Oh, the romance of those names. This was 1950. We would drive down to the film studios in the big BBC Humber Super Snipe, with the recording equipment replacing the back seat. This was before magnetic tape, so we would cut discs. I was mesmerised by the lacquer spiralling off the disc as it recorded our voices.

One of the youth programmes was called *Under-Twenty Review*, in which four young people and an adult critic reviewed the week's art offerings. I became the chairman and did it every week for a year. This helped to compensate for my lack of education. Each week I would see a play – no longer up in the gods but down there in the stalls. There would be a book to read, the latest film to watch, an opera to see. My fee went up to seven guineas a week. I was rolling in it.

I had several of my short essays published in the *Manchester Guardian*, as it was then. I felt like a proper writer, but I was winging it, hoping not to be found out.

My school friend Barrie Vince was the cleverest boy ever, so consequently was despised as a swot. Actually, he didn't swot; it all came so easily to him. He wanted to be an orchestral conductor, but music was just about the only thing he was no good at. We imagined making films. We would write them together, I would direct, and he would score them.

We borrowed an 8mm camera, but we could never decide on the story. It was about a girl running away from something, but we never decided what. We made some images of her in jeopardy, and Barrie chose some dramatic music, which we played against the images on a gramophone. This was our fantasy. Film-making was a distant dream and occupied people who went to Oxford.

Barrie won a scholarship to study law. He got a grant to buy the books he would need but spent that money on music lessons instead. There he met a piano student, Pat, and we both fell in love with her. The three of us were inseparable, *Jules et Jim*. We went to the final rehearsals of the Proms and studiously followed the scores, aping the opening sequence of *The Red Shoes*. We were electrified by Furtwängler and amused by Beecham. I got tickets from the BBC to everything. Barrie and I dazzled Pat with our clever conversation. We were probably insufferable. She was a sexual rubber ball bouncing between us.

After the war and the drab years that followed, this was a glorious flowering. We witnessed the stirrings of the new socialist theatre and the nascent 'Free Cinema' movement. Only the shadow of conscription hung over us. I was now eighteen, and the call-up could come any day.

The National Film Theatre opened on the South Bank. Waiting for the call to arms, I spent my days there, hidden in the dark, hoping to be overlooked. They showed the great silent classics in

magical silver-nitrate black and white to a piano accompaniment –
Griffith's *Birth of a Nation* and *Intolerance*, Abel Gance's *Napoleon*,
von Stroheim's *Greed*, Eisenstein's *Battleship Potemkin*. Barrie and
I sat in the front row, with Pat between us, as the glorious images
drenched us.

Here was a new way of telling stories with images, and I yearned
to learn it. Because there was no language barrier, the silent movie
had swept all before it and conquered the world. D. W. Griffith
believed it was the universal language promised in the Bible that
would bring about the millennium.

I DESCRIBED MY army experience in the film *Queen and Country*.
The brutal training (derived from the First World War) was designed to break us down into automata who would follow orders
so obediently that we would climb out of the trench and walk
towards the machine guns shooting at us, just as our fathers had
done. We conscripts were going to help our American allies fight
the Chinese in the Korean War. Most of the boys I trained with
were posted out there, and some lost their lives. Because I was able
to type, thanks to my mother's gift of a typewriter, I was ignobly
assigned to teach others how to tap for the army.

I was also given the task of lecturing Korea-bound troops on
the history of the war. The son of the socialist MP Ian Mikardo
refused to go on the grounds that I had shown it to be an immor-
al war. I was arrested and charged with 'seducing a soldier from
the course of his duty'. I surrendered my lecture notes, which
were all drawn from reports in *The Times*, the solemn organ of
the Establishment, and my court martial was quietly dropped.

After my two years' conscription, I got a job as a trainee assistant film editor at the newly established television production company ITN. I was fortunate to serve under an inspired editor, Brian Lewis. He was an instinctive manipulator of images. Just then, Karel Reisz published a book, *The Technique of Film Editing*. I read it and gave it to Brian, who was surprised to discover there was a theory of editing. He was so inhibited by it that he couldn't cut for a week. Much later, I got to know Karel and discovered that he had written it before he had gained any actual experience of film-making. It was pure theory.

Television was expanding fast, and within eighteen months I was made an editor myself. A year later, I was directing and editing short documentaries. I took on Barrie Vince as my assistant and taught him the craft I had so recently learnt myself. He had abandoned his musical ambitions but wanted to be involved in the film-making process. He went on to cut several movies and was soon teaching film editing at the National Film School. So it goes.

Film arrived with the twentieth century and swept the world. Four years after arriving in Hollywood, Charlie Chaplin was the most famous and highest-paid man on the planet. The movies are only a little more than a hundred years old. I have been making them for fifty years, so the actors and directors I met early on, the ones coming to the end of their careers at that time, had known the ones who started it all. What a revolution it was, conjuring our stories and dreams onto celluloid and projecting them onto a screen.

THE FILM-MAKING PROCESS

Why are so many people, like Barrie and me, drawn to film-making, when the conditions are often harsh and the hours long? Most of us in the West live comfortable lives, and we are seldom tested. Unconsciously, we yearn to be pressed to our limits, to learn how far we can go, who we are, how we will behave under duress. On the set we lean on each other, support one another. Deep bonds of affection grow up and we become part of a tribe. When, as part of the preparation for the making of *The Emerald Forest*, I lived with a Stone Age tribe in the Xingu region of the Amazon, I came to understand how the tribespeople saw themselves as part of a whole rather than as separate beings, and how our fixation on individuality is so alienating.

However clear your vision, you cannot make a movie on your own. You need a tribe. As a director you struggle to communicate to the cast and crew the essential nature of the film you are making. If things go well, there comes a magical moment when they all 'get' what you are trying to achieve. From that moment, the film makes itself. Your struggle is over and the burden is shared. The pleasure of being part of a group of people bonded by a single purpose, all working at their limits, is exhilarating.

How can we learn the techniques involved in this process? When I was growing up, there was only one film school I knew about. It was in Poland, and it nurtured some fine directors, Roman Polanski among them. Roman is exactly my age, but our paths were very different. I was an apprentice. My first job was joining film on a Bell and Howell editing machine, scraping off the emulsion, applying the heady, volatile cement, then pressing the

9

two strips of film together. I wheedled my way into Brian Lewis's favour, making myself indispensable. Brian had an instinctive way of cutting, so quick and elegant. It was like dance. He knew the language that I had to learn.

Within a year I got a job in television as a film editor myself, cutting short films for current affairs programmes. I proposed ideas and was sent out to direct them, as well as editing them. On one occasion the cameraman failed to arrive, so I took over. I became fascinated by lenses. I had read Isaac Newton's book, *Opticks*, and was fascinated by the behaviour of light, particularly how it passed through the glass elements of the lens and then reacted with the film emulsion.

Movies are made of light.

These short factual films for television gradually got longer. I moved to the BBC, where I made many full-length documentaries. Eventually, frustrated by the limitations of actuality, I began to dramatise, introducing actors and writing dialogue. The BBC allowed me to experiment, encouraged it. By the time I made my first feature film, I was versed in technique and could paint with light. I could speak the language, not fluently, but well enough to function.

Apprenticeship was the traditional way of progressing. Alfred Hitchcock was an art director, David Lean an editor, Nic Roeg a cameraman. Cameramen can trace their lineage back to Griffith's man, Billy Bitzer, for they all rise through the ranks. They start as a clapper-loader, move up to focus-puller, watch and learn from the camera operator, and finally aspire to the lighting skills of a director of photography.

John Wayne was a props man. John Ford made him a star. Elia Kazan asked Ford for advice when he moved from theatre to film. 'Never hire a New York actor,' was Ford's cryptic way of saying film acting is different from theatre acting. However, Kazan did hire NY actors – Marlon Brando, Rod Steiger, Eva Marie Saint – and transformed film acting. Robert De Niro and Al Pacino are heirs of that tradition.

Today, film schools proliferate. There are hundreds of them. In addition, every university has a course on the moving image. Some are better than others. When I first met Martin Scorsese, he was a student at New York University, a school that has high standards. My granddaughter Daphne was at a lesser one. She phoned me in tears. She had to put in a script for a ten-minute film and was in despair. She explained the limitations and the parameters. I wrote it and emailed it to her, in time for the deadline the next morning. Her teachers rejected it as unimaginative and technically naive. My grandson Kit, at a recent summer film course at the University of Southern California, called me to say his script for his short film had been ridiculed. He sent it to me. I thought it wildly original. Despite my failure in helping Daphne, I urged him to stick with it. Entitled *Kick Can*, it showed his hero kicking a Coke can down the street. A boy watches and follows him, kicking his own can. Soon hundreds of boys follow him, kicking their own cans. It was about crowd mentality. No dialogue, just the sound of cans being kicked. It made me think about the grammar of the movies.

Griffith and his cameraman, Billy Bitzer, devised a grammar for film story-telling which we all – makers and watchers – under-stand. For instance, in an intercutting dialogue scene between two people, if one looks camera left and the other camera right, they appear to be looking at each other. This is merely a convention that we have come to accept. Similarly, if two armies are about to engage in battle, one must be charging left to right, the other right to left. If this rule is obeyed, we know they are about to clash. In *Birth of a Nation*, Griffith invented the full-length epic film, with great battle scenes interspersed with intimate human stories, and characters that developed over the course of the film. He opened it in a legitimate theatre with a full orchestra and had men behind the screen doing sound effects. The emotional effect was so powerful that audience members ran into the street telling strangers that they had seen the face of God.

Despite the help offered by the masters of the past, film remains a language that is easy to understand but hard to speak.

I put the techniques of silent-film story-telling that I absorbed from those early masterpieces to work in *Hell in the Pacific*, the tale of two men – Lee Marvin, an American pilot, and Toshiro Mifune, a Japanese naval officer – enemies, marooned on a tiny island in the Pacific. Since they lacked a common language, dialogue could not be used to advance the plot. The story had to be told in images.

Hitchcock, starting in the silent era and later moving to sound, said that when he and his writer finished the script, they would, at that point, go back and put in the dialogue.

The starting point of a movie is not the script but the idea. Since the people at the Hollywood studios who make the decisions are mostly executives working for corporations, they are not expected to have original ideas, so they draw their subjects from best-selling novels or plays, or by remaking hit movies. The executive's fear of failure is much greater than their desire for success. They need people to blame, because most films fail to make money or, at best, break even. The industry is kept afloat by the hit movies that make so much money they keep the whole precarious system afloat. The great morose French producer, Paul Rassam, expressed this dilemma thus: 'In human births, 94 per cent are healthy, 5 per cent have some minor defect, 1 per cent die. With movies, it is the other way round.'

The auteur is one who is able to make films that come from their own imagination or experience and whose films are successful enough to encourage financiers to put up the money they need. These are few indeed. The rest must play a dangerous game with the studios, accepting the projects they are offered but gradually and subtly developing them into their own themes and styles. The studio executives will bombard the director with script notes as a means of retaining the studio's aims and will not give the green light until the director has incorporated their intentions into the script. Once shooting starts, the director, with the help of the actors, can to some extent steer it back to his or her early hopeful intentions, but the executives are watching the daily rushes and will demand reshoots if he or she deviates too far from the agreed script. It is a war of attrition.

The decision to commit a great deal of money towards making a movie is not made lightly. More and more, the advertising and distribution arms are influencing those decisions. Mainstream American films are sold via thirty-second TV ads, so the key question is: how do you express each movie in thirty seconds? They will argue that if it is not possible to get the idea across in that time, then it should not be made. A well-known star toting a gun or kissing another movie star will tell audiences what they need to know. They have seen it all before. Sequels are easy to sell for the same reason, hence their proliferation. The enemy is originality. How to sell something unfamiliar to audiences in thirty seconds? Consequently, Hollywood movies have a tendency to look alike, to be predictable.

Every studio buys the film rights of books, plays, magazine articles. They finance scripts written from this source material, often getting them rewritten by other writers. The studios make one out of twenty of these projects. They will also consider scripts written by successful screenwriters and submitted by important agents. Unsolicited scripts are mostly not read. There are just too many of them.

If the odds are so stacked against you, why bother to write a script? It's because we can't help it; it's because the movies are us and our subconscious and our dreams, and we can't help it. We have to do it, or try to. Committing yourself to the life of a film-maker is to embrace a form of joyous slavery.

Occasionally, a film student will make a ten-minute graduation film that is so dazzling a studio will give them a picture. They will then hem them in with a dominating producer, a cameraman who has been trying for years to direct and a barrage of notes, all aimed at weeding out the originality that first attracted them. So most young writers or directors must take the independent route when starting out. Many countries have a film board or office, supported by the government, that will give loans or grants to movies. There are also tax shelters that will invest in films. The major American studios have subsidiaries, like Sony Classics or Fox Searchlight, which will pick up independent films for distribution and sometimes invest in them. Most independent films have to be made for less than $5 million. The limited distribution they can achieve will not support a greater budget.

The heartening fact is that, somehow or other, and against all the odds, a few really good films get made every year, and once in a decade a film arrives that seems to reinvent cinema. Stanley Kubrick's *2001: A Space Odyssey* was such a movie, and now, in 2019, we have another, *Roma*. Its director, Alfonso Cuarón, has had big hits in conventional cinema and earned the support to make a more personal film. He elected to make a movie about his own middle-class family in Mexico City, in black and white, in the Spanish language, with no stars, and with the maid, Cleo, as the central character – a set of ingredients that would guarantee its rejection by any studio anywhere.

It gets worse. Cuarón tears up D. W. Griffith's film grammar, which we all live by, and reinvents the cinema. The camera sits at a discreet distance, and except for some subtle pans, scarcely moves. There are no close-ups. His blocking and choreography are impeccable. He brings everything to life. It envelops us. We become that family, our faith in cinema restored.

The Script – Writing

Alfonso Cuarón clearly didn't listen to the script gurus who will tell you how to write scripts in the form that studios respond to. They will instruct you to divide your script into three acts and weed out the originality that will frighten the executives. David Lean split his scripts into ten ten-minute reels (and more reels than that for his epic movies). He trained as an editor, and editors break down a picture into reels. They work and polish every one. Each of them, said Lean, should have one great scene, develop character, advance the narrative and give the audience time to take a breath, dropping back to a landscape or showing a flowing river, which always suggests progress. With digital editing there are no reels, so infinite changes can be made speedily and muddled shooting rescued.

Seduce your viewers, let your images lure them into the movie, making them lose their hold on life and disappear into your story. Reward them and serve them, as Cuarón does.

However original your script may be, lay it out using a

computer program called Final Draft. It will make your screenplay look serious and professional, and will conceal your covert intentions. Final Draft, for all its merits, is poorly named. There is no final draft. The writing process continues throughout the making and editing of the movie. Film is fluid; it evolves. Every time you cast an actor, it alters. Some actors fall below your expectations, others soar above them. The balance changes, and you follow the inspired actor wherever they will take you. You hang on to your vision, but sometimes you must change too. A movie gathers power as it progresses. It develops its own momentum, and you are advised to serve its needs rather than drag it back to what you thought it was. When the film is cut together, let the actors review and modify their performances using Automatic Dialogue Replacement (ADR). This process allows you to add and alter lines, cut superfluous ones and improve performances. The writing goes on to the end.

Tom Stoppard wrote the screenplay of *Empire of the Sun* for Steven Spielberg. He discovered that they had brought in another writer. When he viewed the film, he could not detect any new or changed scenes. He asked the producer, Kathleen Kennedy, what the other writer had contributed. She said, 'The crew cut and the leather jacket.' This was the image that told us the boy had grown up and adapted. He was no longer a British schoolboy, he had become an American. Tom said he had no idea such things were the province of the writer. 'My scripts are just compromised plays,' he said. This was long before *Shakespeare in Love*, where his sparkling dialogue was woven skilfully into the movie fabric.

Tom and I wrote a script together once. Like so many others, it was never made. This was before the computer, before Final Draft, which, among other wonders, allows you to shift scenes around at will. We were 'scissors-and-pasting'. The pages were spread out on the floor as we cut and pasted them into new positions. 'I guess this is screenwriting,' said Tom, wielding the paste brush.

The best option is to write the script yourself. Second best is to co-write it. Third is to at least shape its rhythm and architecture. Not to write the script at all is to interpret someone else's vision, but why would you suffer all the sacrifices, humiliations and contumely merely to do that?

A writer I have worked with a great deal over the last forty years is Rospo Pallenberg. He is half Italian and studied architecture in Rome. We collaborated on *Excalibur, The Emerald Forest, The Heretic* and several more projects that did not get made. We spent a year together writing *The Lord of the Rings* for United Artists, but the cost frightened them away.

I wrote the first draft of *Excalibur*. It was long and sprawling. I was determined to tell the legend in its entirety, from the birth of King Arthur to the quest for the Holy Grail, whereas most writers have wisely opted for one part of it – Camelot or Arthur's youth. When I began to despair of condensing the story into the span of a single movie, I sent my draft to Rospo, who applied his massive mind to the problem and made it work, compressing the elements of the myth together. I then polished his draft, but he had built the architecture and established the through-line of the story.

This was untypical of our collaborations. We usually locked ourselves in a room and invented and argued. He always defended his ideas doggedly and would fight to keep them in the script. We are close friends and love spending time together, but our sensibilities are very different. The scripts I write alone are sparse, just notes to myself, whereas Rospo's are almost stiflingly detailed. He writes as though he were making them director-proof. That directors find it difficult to engage with his screenplays is probably the reason why so many of them have not been made. Rospo did not go to school until he was eleven. He played on his own and never had to share his toys. Avoiding school meant that his imagination was not beaten out of him and is responsible for his original way of thinking. I have just read his script about Buddy Bolden and the birth of jazz. It is a great, sprawling masterwork, an anthem for the birth of a nation.

Writing collaborations take many forms. Robert Bolt and David Lean worked very closely together, but David always typed up the scenes. Billy Wilder, when asked how he worked with his writer, I. A. L. Diamond, said, 'He writes down the words, and I go into the cage.'

I was staying in the Hôtel Raphael, in Paris. Jean-Pierre Melville called on me. He admired *Deliverance* and arrived in his open-topped Rolls-Royce to take me on a tour of the Paris locations where famous movies had been shot. He came up to my room wearing his signature Stetson.

'I write my script in your room,' he said.

I thought he must be mangling the English language. 'You write your scripts in your room?'

'No, I write my script in your room.'

It turned out that he had indeed written what was to be his final film, *Un flic*, in that very hotel room. His method was to lock himself in, have his meals sent up, and each evening his secretary would knock and he would slide his pages under the door for her to type up. He would not emerge until the script was finished. When writing alone you need to find a way of avoiding distractions.

Walter Donohue

If you write alone, there comes a point when you have to expose your script to the world. While mine were still tender, I would show them only to Walter Donohue, a painfully honest but sympathetic critic.

Walter came to England to avoid the Vietnam draft. He became the dramaturge at the Royal Shakespeare Company. When Channel 4 opened, he worked at Film 4 and guided a number of films onto the screen. One of the first was Neil Jordan's *Angel*, which I produced. Walter came over to Ireland and followed that film through its production. We became firm friends.

He moved to Faber & Faber, where he became an editor, specialising in film books. We founded *Projections* together, an annual journal about the film-making process. We invited directors, designers and actors to write about their methods, publishing thirteen editions. Walter did most of the hard work. It remains a unique record of contemporary film-making. Each year we posed a question to directors around the world. One time we asked: what film would you make if you had an unlimited budget and time? Most were appalled by the prospect. Limitations force you to invent solutions. Pressure often reveals truth. Up to a point. If the strictures are too severe, the film falls apart.

Walter lives alone in a kind of zen state. His living room is quite bare but for a pyramid of stones in its centre. He traverses London on his scooter, covering long distances. Somehow he manages to see every important movie and read every book that counts, and he knows everybody of worth. He is modest and unassuming, yet at ease with talent and unimpressed by celebrity.

I am lucky to be one of his coterie of authors and film-makers whom he guides and nurtures. He appears in the end credits of many movies. It usually says, 'With thanks to Walter Donohue.'

I put my tentative scripts into his safe hands. He points out weak points and makes considered suggestions. He never enthuses or condemns. He simply enters the story as a sympathetic friend and stays with it right through to its release. He will make a casting suggestion that you never thought of. He somehow puts himself in a position where it is very difficult to praise him. He is a kind of secular priest, a father confessor. Recently, his many admirers gave him a surprise party to celebrate his contributions. He was astonished that we would do such a thing.

So my advice to screenwriters is: find a Walter Donohue.

The Script – Preparing to Shoot

I am often asked by first-time directors, 'How do you know where to put the camera?' If you have written the scene properly, the camera position will choose itself.

For instance, we're in a working-class apartment. A stressed woman is washing dishes. A baby is crying. A man enters the front door and calls out to his wife. Depending on how you write this scene, you are automatically selecting the camera position.

(a) A woman is washing dishes. She is stressed. She cringes when a baby cries. A man calls her name. He appears over her shoulder. He takes her in his arms.

Camera on woman's back – all one shot.

(b) A baby cries; track in on its roaring open mouth. A woman washing dishes turns towards the sound of the baby. She cringes.

A man enters from the front door. We pan him to the woman, and he wraps her in his arms.

(1) Camera close on baby. (2) Side angle on woman as she turns towards baby. (3) Close on man as he enters door. Pan and track him to woman.

(c) A man enters the apartment. He frowns at the sound of a crying baby. He sees his wife's back as she washes dishes in the kitchen. He shakes his head, goes into the bedroom and picks up the baby.

(1) Man enters door. (2) His POV of woman. (3) Pan man to baby.

Of course, there are many choices within those plans – the lens, the height of the camera, the light source – depending on the mood and atmosphere you are seeking, but in each case the camera position is obvious and inevitable.

'How do you know where to point the camera?' Sam Mendes once asked Conrad Hall, the late, great director of photography (DP).

'I point it at the story,' he replied.

If you have to ask the DP where to point the camera, you are not a director. Your job, among many other tasks, is to choose the lens, design the composition and define the camera movement. The DP's job is to offer suggestions and execute your choices.

Don't make the script too good. The more cinematic a script, the harder it is to read. A script has to be written for producers and financiers, many of whom are visually illiterate, but don't let them see the shooting script. It would frighten them to death. Ingmar Bergman's scripts were sparsely written, and on his copy he would put a number against each scene – 2 or 4 or 3 – to remind himself how many set-ups he would need.

Time your script. If it comes out too long, rewrite it. It is easier and cheaper to cut a script than an over-long film. If the first cut of your film comes out at four hours, it means that 50 per cent of what you have shot will be junked. If you had timed it properly, you could have shot it in half the time or spent twice the time on the scenes you have ended up with. Put the timings against each scene and stick to them when shooting.

Why do people so often say, 'I loved it, but it was too long'? It is because the director had a good story and cast, which he could not quite liberate from the dross clinging to the movie. Strip out everything from the script that's not intended.

You'd be well advised to choose a 'genre' movie for your first film. A thriller is a safe bet. Tension and suspense will always grip an audience. Within its familiar framework, you can explore your characters and take them into bizarre or beautiful settings. Hitchcock said, 'A man gets out of bed, takes a shower, dresses. It is boring. Put at the beginning of the scene a shot of a rifle aimed at him, and all those banal actions become fascinating.'

'All you need to make a movie is a girl and a gun,' said Jean-Luc Godard; in other words, sex and violence, the primary colours of the medium.

The eye generalises; the camera is specific. A London street on a dull November day: the eye will see total greyness. If you photograph it, a red bus will jump out at you. The camera has the innocent eye of a child, seeing everything fresh, which is why 'coming-of-age' movies work well.

You have to be brave to try comedy as a first film. It is probably the most difficult form. The writing, the casting, the pacing are fiendishly hard to pull off. A story drawn from your own life can be appealing and its honesty touching, but you must take care of the narrative drive to keep your audience connected. As a first film this kind of movie is a 'calling card' – not expected to find a big audience, but a way to demonstrate your skills and encourage financiers to offer you further pictures.

Nobody sets out to make a bad film, but most turn out that way. So many things can go wrong – lack of chemistry in the cast, bad weather, money running out, sluggish pace, getting the zeitgeist wrong – but the one thing that all successful movies have in common is . . . luck. So cross your fingers. We always know when we are watching a great movie, because there comes a point when we don't want it to end.

Beauty is beguiling but can betray a director by slowing down the movie. 'Kill your darlings.' As a DP once said to me, 'You have to be careful as a cameraman. One good shot can ruin a bad film.' Consistency is vital.

Whenever I mentor a first-time director, I oblige them to story-board the entire film. This makes them see it in images. Breaking the scenes down into shots will tell them how many set-ups they need. Inevitably, there will be more than they will have time to shoot, so they will need to do a second draft, bringing the number of shots down to earth. A feature film will average eight to twelve set-ups a day. If a director boasts of doing twenty to thirty a day, they are stealing time from the actors and the lighting. Light is paramount. It is what films are made of, so nurse it, revere it. Film is the art of the possible. A forty-day shoot will get you around four hundred and fifty set-ups. No one has ever had enough time or money to shoot an ambitious film.

With your first assistant director and production manager you will lay out a shooting schedule. Your budget will determine how many shooting days you can afford. You must shoehorn your scenes into that. The schedule offers you another way of examining your script. Is that scene worth the two shooting days that it seems to require? Maybe you should rewrite it in a simpler form. Faced with necessity, you can sometimes find a single image that will replace a whole scene.

So you have your script. The clearer you have the film in your head, the harder it is to cast, because no actor can quite match your invented characters. Sometimes they can improve on your ideal; more often they will fall short. Change the part to suit the actor. It never works the other way round.

Rehearsal

If possible, you should assemble your cast and do a reading of the script. You, the director, must read the directions and have each actor read their part. I always ask the actors to read their lines flat, rather than act them. If you record this process, by listening back to it you can learn a great deal about your dialogue. You can then tailor the lines to the actors.

The next step is to make a rehearsal schedule, so that you can work with actors who have scenes together. It is a mistake to act the scenes out because, when you're shooting, the actors will try to reproduce the effect they achieved in rehearsal. It will feel second-hand. All you need to do is discuss the intentions of the scene, its place in the story, how it should develop the characters, and its emotional temperature. In this way you avoid the problem of actors arriving on the set with an erroneous notion of what the scene is about.

Shooting

Miraculously, you have somehow got backing for your script and a green light.

Preparation is vital. Do as much of it as you can. Prep is cheaper than shooting. In choosing locations, work out how much time you will lose travelling from one to another. Find locations that are closer together. Make a shot list for each day and give it to the DP and first assistant director, then everyone will know what to do and can prepare in advance. Look at the scenes you have to shoot that day and work out how they can be covered by the twelve set-ups you can expect to make. At the end of each day give the DP the first set-up for the next morning. Phil Lathrop, the DP of *Point Blank*, said, 'All directors think a lot about how to shoot a scene, but very few think it through.'

You will be confronted with a daily avalanche of choices that need instant decisions. When you first start out, you need to convince the cast and crew that you know what you are doing by being decisive. It is better to make the wrong decision than not make one at all. Impetus is everything. Only when you have had a few successes can you afford the luxury of changing your mind. If the scene is clear in your head, you can eliminate set-ups you won't need. When directors shoot a lot of angles and takes, the actors start thinking, 'Well, this one probably won't be in the picture.' They lose focus. Get the actors used to giving everything in the first take, not using the first five takes as rehearsal. If they believe that everything you shoot will be in the picture, they will concentrate and husband their energy.

When you have a good printed take, do one more at a quicker pace. It often turns out to be the one you use.

Just before you say 'action', it is good to adjust an out-of-place hair on an actor's head, whether it is or isn't. The actor will think, 'My God, he is watching everything. I am safe in his hands.'

'Presence' in an actor means just that – they are wholly present and not partially elsewhere. Few can achieve this; most children and all great movie stars can.

An experienced actor, uncertain of an untried director's skill, will opt for 'survival acting' – 'I know how to get through this scene without making a fool of myself.' You need to earn an actor's trust before they will jump off the cliff or open their heart.

The space between actors in a two-shot should coincide with their emotional closeness or distance.

Strip out everything that is inessential or unintended in each set-up. As the audience subconsciously come to realise that everything in every frame is relevant, they will fall into your grip and sense your power (vide any late Kubrick picture).

Make up your mind: the camera can represent the hero's or a God's-eye point of view, seeing everything from all angles. Choose one and stay with it. Audiences will follow you if you set out the rules from the beginning and stick to them. Inconsistency is fatal.

You can shoot a scene in a single complex shot or break it down into several shots that will cut together. Ask yourself this question: which method will express the emotions and tell the story more effectively?

Film reels last only ten or, at most, twenty minutes. Digital allows a shot to last much longer than that. With *Rope*, Hitchcock attempted to make a film that felt like a single shot (the joins were concealed). This creates tension because the audience believes it is happening in real time. Alejandro González Iñárritu tried the same trick in *Birdman*, which took place in a theatre, with long, carefully choreographed takes and concealed cuts. He explored the technique further in *The Revenant*. More recently, the German director Sebastian Schipper made *Victoria* (a night out that ends in a bank heist) in real time and a single shot. If there are concealed cuts, no one has spotted them. Multiple takes and coverage from many angles are for directors who haven't worked out what a scene is about and hope they can solve it in the cutting room, leaving a mess for the editor.

A second camera can be useful for an action scene, but in other circumstances it merely compromises the lighting.

Use close-ups sparingly for emotional emphasis. You get diminishing returns from their overuse. Never do a close-up of eyes. We read emotion in the way eyes relate to the whole face.

A cut should either make a point of emphasis or succeed in concealing itself. If it does neither, it is a failure.

If all this advice sounds dogmatic, let me point out that many good movies have been made employing methods that are different from the one I favour. There are many ways of skinning a cat, but you must have a cat.

When I teach, I pin up a copy of Magritte's painting of a pipe, under which he writes, '*Ceci n'est pas une pipe*' – 'This is not a pipe.' It is futile to strive for reality. Film is not life; film is metaphor. Ingmar Bergman expressed it well: 'I am not trying to make it real,' he said. 'I am trying to make it alive.'

Film at its highest level is close to the condition of dreaming. It connects to the unconscious, as dreams do. It takes the physical (actors, sets, landscapes, equipment, money) and turns it into light. Material into spirit. Alchemy. You spend all those millions, and at the end of the day all you have is light flickering on a wall.

*

WHAT IS THE FUTURE OF FILM? Terrence Malick made *The Tree of Life* as a succession of beautiful images linking a family to the natural world around them. There is only one conventional sequence in the entire film: a cross-cutting dialogue scene. If God made a home movie, it would look something like this. The images and acting are beguiling, but the absence of narrative drive means that if the spell falters, Malick loses his hold on us. As with Andrei Tarkovsky, I watch his films in a heightened state of excitement and drowsiness. A great revelation is about to manifest itself, yet I fear I will fall asleep and miss it. Malick and Tarkovsky dare to engage with the metaphysical. They have taken film to the very edge of what is possible.

HOLLYWOOD – BURT REYNOLDS, LEE MARVIN

D. W. Griffith and his cameraman, Billy Bitzer, invented the language of film while thousands were dying in the trenches of the First World War. I spent months immersed in Griffith's films for a documentary I made on him for the BBC in 1965. Griffith believed that film would unite the people of the world. Alas, that failed to occur, but the myths that grew up around the movies and their stars became woven into our dreams.

When people discover that I was in Hollywood in the mid-1960s, they often ask if I ever met Marilyn Monroe. Sadly, I did not. She died a year before I arrived. The closest I got to her was her ex-husband, Arthur Miller. Arthur wrote great plays, but did he ever shrug off the status of being Marilyn's husband? His late play, *After the Fall*, has as its central character a woman much like Marilyn. Her myth was too strong and the play could not compete with it, just as Chaplin never quite escaped the little tramp.

I asked Billy Wilder what it was like to direct Marilyn. A dream and a nightmare, he said, but not in that order. I knew she was notorious for being late. Billy was once asked if her tardiness upset him. Famously, he said, 'No, I always wanted to read *War and Peace*, but I never had time before.' Marilyn got upset about his witty jibes and called his home. Billy's wife answered, receiving a barrage of abuse about her husband: 'You tell that son of a bitch to stop trashing me.' Then Marilyn said, sweetly, 'And all my best to you, Audrey.' Norma Jean saw Marilyn Monroe as an impersonation that she was quite good at.

One of the first people I met in Hollywood was Christopher Isherwood. He had met them all – Marilyn, Chaplin, James Dean,

Marlene Dietrich – and I plied him with questions. Greta Garbo was a neighbour of his in the Santa Monica Canyon. She would drop in at night wanting to go for moody walks. When he didn't feel up to it, he would hide behind his sofa.

'You would hide behind your sofa to avoid Greta Garbo?' I said reprovingly.

Of all the couples I met when I arrived in Hollywood, Isherwood and Don Bachardy were one of the few whose relationship endured. They were together for thirty years. Isherwood wrote in his diary every day to convince himself he was real in that insubstantial town. When Chris died, Don read those diaries backwards. He said to me, 'I am longing to get back to the date when Chris and I met, so that I can find out who I was.'

WE RENTED A HOUSE in Malibu Colony while I was making *Point Blank*. It was 1966. Our twins, Daisy and Charley, were only two months old. My wife, Christel, would wheel them up and down the little private road. Cary Grant had fathered a child with Dyan Cannon, but they were already estranged. A nanny would bring out their baby, Jennifer, and prop her up in the seat next to her father, and Grant would slowly drive up and down in his Rolls-Royce before returning her to the nanny. He and Christel would compare babies. Grant famously came from Bristol, where I had worked for the BBC, but I never found the courage to say, 'Mr Archie Leach, don't you miss the Clifton Suspension Bridge?' I wonder if a scrap of Archie was left in Grant's invented persona.

Jamie Lee Curtis is one of the most original characters I have ever met, yet her name is a fiction. It acknowledges her mother, Janet Leigh, and her father, Tony Curtis, yet both her parents' names were invented by the studios' publicity departments, so Jamie's name is a second-generation fiction. Her real name is Helen Schwartz. Her marriage to Christopher Guest meant her name changed again, this time to Lady Haden-Guest.

I met Jimmy Stewart once. I gushed about his brilliant performances. 'If you think I am that good,' he said, 'why have you never cast me?' He was terse, perhaps tired of being the nice guy he played on screen.

I was seated next to Dan Rather, the CBS news anchor, at a New York dinner party, and we spoke about the effects of notoriety on the famous people we had known. I said that fame had stolen Elvis Presley's identity. I found him acutely embarrassed at being Elvis. Marlon Brando despised the actor Brando. Acting is just a bunch of tricks, he assured me, not proper work for a man.

Just then a man entered the room. 'Do you know who that is?' said Dan. 'James Watson – Crick and Watson – the guys who discovered DNA, the double helix.'

Here was a man who had changed our understanding of human life, solved one of the great mysteries. He ranked alongside Newton and Einstein. I gushed even more than I had with Jimmy Stewart. I almost curtsied. I waited for his words, for his wisdom, for revelation. Alas, what he said was, 'What was it like working with Burt Reynolds?' It was one of the most disappointing moments of my life. How could genius be buried in the banal?

In mitigation, after *Deliverance*, Burt had done a nude centre-fold in *Cosmopolitan* and was very much in the news. He had become a sex symbol. Burt found this a burden. He told me that women expected something amazing from their experiences with him. 'But', he said ruefully, 'I'm just a fumbler like everyone else.'

Burt was nominated for a Best Supporting Actor Oscar for *Boogie Nights*. He was the hot favourite. Everyone agreed that he deserved it, not only for the part, but in recognition of his entire, very successful career. When the winner was declared, they showed the four losers bravely applauding – or three of them, for Burt's face was twisted in agonised disappointment. Jon Voight, his brave comrade in *Deliverance*, caught that look and called him at the Four Seasons Hotel, where he was staying. Burt was not taking calls. Understandably, he was lying low. Jon went to the hotel and tried to persuade them to put him through. They explained that Burt had given strict instructions and refused to do so. Jon discovered that Burt and his girlfriend had ordered room service, so he borrowed a waiter's uniform and arrived at their door with his trolley. He knocked, then opened the door with his pass key. The girlfriend was on the phone, and Burt was reading in bed. Jon assumed a French accent and cried out, 'Oh, it eez Burt Reynolds.' He jumped on top of the startled Burt and kissed him. They laughed and talked for hours. That's a friend.

In 2018 Burt died. There was an outpouring of affection and sorrow. I was besieged by the press, seeking tributes. *Deliverance* had rescued him from the grind of TV, and its success launched him onto the talk shows, where his wit and good looks made him welcome and popular.

When we finished shooting *Deliverance*, Burt told me, 'I was in this movie on false pretences, John. You see, I can't act. I was just faking it.' That was both funny and partially true. Oddly, Brando described film acting – lending part of yourself to a character – to me as fake. Daniel Day-Lewis believed that it was essential to *become* the character you were playing and to totally suppress your own identity. It would take him a year to recover his own identity and throw off the assumed character, which is why he works so infrequently. Jon Voight wanted to find the truth of a scene, but Burt had no interest in the truth, only a version of it that would make people laugh or make himself look good.

When I worked with him, Burt was a 'survival actor' (i.e. 'I know how to get through this scene without making a fool of myself'), but Jon was a method actor and wanted to analyse every scene in excruciating detail. They worked well together. Jon made Burt think, and Burt made Jon get on with it.

The male rape scene in *Deliverance* was carefully worked out by the two actors, Ned Beatty and Bill McKinney, who played the mountain man. I designed it in terms of what would be seen and not seen. Burt repeatedly told the story that McKinney was so caught up in it that he was about to enter Ned, when he, Burt, rushed in and pulled him off. In fact, Burt was not present when the scene was shot. He was not called that day, since his character does not appear until after the rape scene.

There is a story I have often repeated of a dinner with Lee Marvin on Venice Pier. Lee got very drunk, and I insisted on driving his car. We struggled over the keys, and when I eventually prevailed, to save face he would not get in the car but climbed up onto the roof, refusing to come down. It was late at night, but he lived only a few miles down the Pacific Coast Highway, so I drove carefully along it. I was pulled over by a cop, who moved over to my window, looked up and said, 'Do you know you've got Lee Marvin on your roof?'

I was surprised to find the story in Burt's autobiography, with Burt at the wheel instead of me. The story was just too good not to borrow it – or had Burt told it so often that he had come to believe it?

Lee was a great film actor and a truth-seeker, however painful. *Point Blank* was a *pas de deux*, he the brilliant dancer, I the choreographer. He was also an alcoholic. I once asked him why so many actors were drunks.

'Maybe it's the other way round,' he said.

This was Lee at his most gnomic. I asked for an explanation.

'If you're a drunk, there are not too many jobs you can hold down,' he said.

Fame is a confirmation of identity, an escape from anonymity, but it seldom corresponds to who you are. Lee Marvin, however, was always Lee Marvin, a drunk recovering from the trauma of war.

Lee carried his father's First World War handgun all through the Pacific campaign, hoping it would confer bravery on him. He revered and feared his father. When Lee was drunk, he would sometimes dare to take the gun apart into its many constituent elements, then attempt to put it together again. He seldom could. It had to wait till he was sober. A father and son, fighting in two wars.

When the First World War was declared, my father and his eighteen-year-old classmates marched down to the recruiting centre and joined up. All nineteen became subalterns and perished in the trenches of France; all of them, that is, except for my father – a clerk put a tick against his name and he was sent to India, where he played polo and commanded Gurkhas. He led them into battle against the Turks on horseback, with a drawn sword, but aware of the Gurkhas' reputation the Turks wisely retreated. It was the closest my father got to seeing action.

But for that tick, I would not be telling these stories.

Hope and Glory is based on my childhood memories of the London Blitz. Closely following actual events, the end of the film shows my older sister Wendy, at seventeen, giving birth to Robert, marrying the Canadian soldier who fathered the child and being shipped off to Canada with her baby. It was a year before her husband was demobbed and able to follow her home.

I recently got a call from a man in Montreal, Michel Lejeune, who claimed to be Wendy's son. He had waited until his adopted parents died before he started looking for his birth mother. Under Canadian law at the time it was almost impossible for an adopted child to discover its origins, but, through a university research study on war brides, he had located Wendy, and the trail had led to me. Apparently, in that year before her husband returned to Canada, Wendy had had another child and gave it up for adoption. I had to tell him that Wendy had died a couple of years earlier, but if he wanted to know what she was like, he should rent *Hope and Glory*.

My film *Queen and Country* describes Wendy's return to England and her decision to leave her Canadian husband. After some wild affairs she met Tom, a Cornish boat builder and fisherman sixteen years her junior. They started a relationship which we all expected would be short-lived, but they married and lived happily together for thirty years. Tom was so bereft at her death that he became a recluse.

Wendy had never mentioned this additional child, at least not to me. Did she ever tell her Canadian husband? Or Tom, or her children, Robert and Linda? I was in a quandary. Could I tell them about Michel? If she had never told her family about this child, would it distress them?

My cousin June also lives in Cornwall. I put the case to her. By chance, she had been present on Wendy's eightieth birthday, when she confessed to Tom and her children that she had had another child. She had kept it a secret all those years. Strangely, her confession coincided exactly with the time Michel started looking for her. Who fathered Michel remains a mystery.

That tick against my father's name brought Wendy into being, and some kind of accident led to Michel.

I can see nothing of Wendy's wildness in Michel. He is a gentle, cultivated man, a musician, and he has become a friend. He was photographed next to his half-brother, Robert – less than a year apart in age – and they look like twins. He is delighted to have found his family and his enthusiasm has drawn us all closer together, we who take kin for granted and scarcely meet other than for weddings and funerals. He has taught us to hunker down together. He said it was a lucky chance that he found us. I said it is a lucky chance that any of us are here at all.

Queen and Country continues Wendy's story but is mostly a film about my time as an eighteen-year-old conscript in the army during the Korean War. It is always the young, children really, who are sent off to fight. George Bernard Shaw said the way to end wars would be to pass a law that said only men over forty should be allowed to fight.

In those early 1950s England was suffering the effects of two world wars – only twenty or so years apart – which had killed and wounded millions and brought the country to its knees. Nevertheless, in my brief time in the army we fought the Korean War, the Malay rebels, the Mau Mau in Africa, dealt with an incipient revolt in Cyprus and lived with the fear of nuclear Armageddon with the USSR. Sadly, history tells us that peace occurs as brief interludes between wars. Yuval Noah Harari, the Israeli visionary, tells us that future wars will last not five years but five minutes, as cyber-attacks will cripple nations.

However, we are weary of war and our heroes now are men of peace – Gandhi, Mandela and, most poignantly, a woman, Aung San Suu Kyi. The image of this frail, beautiful woman in her Burmese robes, always with a flower in her hair and armed only with her Buddhist pacifism, confronting the country's brutal military dictators is immensely powerful.

She was always free to leave Burma, to rejoin her husband and sons in England, but if she did so, would not be allowed to return.

She could not abandon her suffering countrymen. Alone, under house arrest, she refused the food supplied by the generals for fear of being poisoned and survived by selling her furniture bit by bit, until only her beloved piano remained. Finally, that had to go too, and her music was silenced.

An American, Alan Clements, had conducted a series of secret interviews with Suu Kyi while she was under arrest. He had smuggled the tapes out of Burma at considerable risk and planned to publish them. I met Alan through Bob Chartoff, whose friendship I celebrate later in this book. Bob was impressed with Alan's brave endeavour and gave him financial succour while he was working on the book. Through Bob I got to know Alan a little. He was a devout Buddhist and had been a monk in Burma for some years. From listening to his interviews with Suu Kyi, I came to understand something of her powerful pacifism and her heroic stand against the brutal generals. Alan was more equivocal. He had been a drug addict and, filled with self-loathing, had gone to Burma to purge himself, as he saw it, of evil.

Consequently, I was most intrigued some time later when a script was sent to me called *Beyond Rangoon*. It was about a woman travelling alone through Burma. She had lost a child and was seeking solace in this healing land, as Alan had done. Her journey coincided with the students' revolt that was brutally put down by the generals, killing hundreds of unarmed youths, some being driven into Inya Lake in Rangoon to drown.

Here was a Manichaean collision of pacifism and violence. Does great goodness draw evil to itself? Or is it that meekness allows evil men to seize power? When the barefoot monks in their saffron robes marched in protest against the generals, they too were gunned down.

Following in my father's bootsteps (for that tick took him to Burma as well), I set out on my journey. At that time, a tourist was only allowed to spend seven days in the country. A taxi drove me past Aung San Suu Kyi's house in Rangoon, where she was under house arrest, but the driver dared not stop.

I went into a roadside café, a wooden shack with dirt floors, and sat at the communal table. A girl of fifteen or so was eating what I came to recognise as the staple diet of the people: rice and a few sparse vegetables. As I sat beside her, she immediately slid her plate towards me and, with an open smile, offered to share it with me. At every turn I was met with kindness and generosity by these impoverished people. The soldiers in their gleaming uniforms were like another race, avatars who had conquered this magical land.

The monks became a familiar sight as they went into the streets each day to beg for their daily bread. Almost every male spends at least a year in a monastery, enduring poverty and humility. I asked an old monk why it was that the Burmese seemed so happy, given their deprivation and subjection. He laughed.

'Why,' he said, 'we are taught that all we can expect from life is pain and suffering, so when something good happens, however small, we are delighted. In the West, you believe that happiness is your birthright, so you are always disappointed.'

I put that line into the movie.

As I travelled, I covertly photographed soldiers so that we could dress our actors correctly when it came to shooting the picture, because clearly I would not be able to make it in Burma. Up in the mountains in the teak forest, I watched foresters selecting a tree to be cut and an elephant drawing it out. How good and measured that looked after the desolation of the clear felling I had witnessed in the Amazon rainforest. This beautiful hardwood will thrive only at high altitudes where it's hot and there's a lot of rain. The leaves of the teak tree are huge – four or five feet wide – and leathery. When the rain hits them, the timpani sound roars through the forest.

One day, on the banks of the Irrawaddy River, the noon sun was beating down, so impulsively I stripped off and plunged in. I was ambushed by the force of the current and swept downstream some three hundred yards before I managed to climb out. Under a grove of trees sat a platoon of soldiers nursing their weapons and sheltering from the blistering heat. They watched a naked, white-skinned man clamber clumsily out of the river a few feet from where they sat. These were men who raped and pillaged. They looked to their officer for guidance. He glared at me but gave no orders. I tried to look dignified as I walked slowly back up the river bank to retrieve my clothes.

The golden domes of the pagodas and temples glittered across the dreamlike landscapes, tributes to the Buddha who had founded the only religion without a god while promising the possibility of enlightenment. What was this enlightenment? I asked the monks. The question always provoked laughter.

'What do you feel about our land?' one monk asked. I replied that I felt a sense of peace and harmony. I said it was a relief not to be a consumer preyed on by advertisers. This caused more laughter. 'We would like to consume more,' one said. 'Begging for food every day is hard work.'

At a tiny English bookshop in Rangoon I found a copy of the novelist Gerald Hanley's book about the British army's fight against the Japanese in the Second World War. Gerry was an old friend who had ended his days at Luggala, Garech Browne's Irish haven in County Wicklow. There he had regaled me with his adventures in India, Africa and elsewhere. Wherever great events had occurred – the partition of India, the dark shadow of the Mau Mau – Gerry had contrived to be there, but he had never mentioned that he was the official military chronicler embedded with the army in Burma.

His book describes how Suu Kyi's father, Aung San, wanted to free Burma from British rule and so went to Japan to study military tactics. He returned with the invading Japanese as a valuable adviser. At the time, the Japanese were building the notorious Burma Road through the jungle with the forced labour of prisoners of war, thousands of whom perished.

Aung San was horrified when he witnessed the cruelty of the Japanese. He defected to the British and fought against his former comrades. The Japanese were feared for their manic bravery, their willingness to die for the emperor, but Gerry describes how a battalion of Nigerians faced up against the Japanese in the jungle.

Responding to the heat, the tall Nigerians were almost naked but for their weapons. The supposedly fearless Japanese, when confronted by these black giants, fled for their lives.

After the war Aung San went to London and negotiated Burma's independence with the British prime minister, Clement Attlee. He returned a conquering hero, only to be assassinated by the predecessors of the generals who ruled the country when we were making the film.

When I was working in television, I made a documentary about Edwina Mountbatten. I was invited into the drawing room of the house she shared with her husband Louis in Hampshire. The butler offered me a silver box of cigarettes, each one embossed with the letters 'MofB', for Dickie, as Edwina called her husband, had commanded the war that saw the recapture of Burma and as a result had been awarded the title Mountbatten of Burma. Edwina chain-smoked. I asked her if she had ever tried to give up the habit. 'I did once,' she said. 'I spoke to God and said, "I will give up smoking if you let my husband win in Burma." So I stopped smoking. Dickie was driven back on all fronts,' she added, 'so I took up smoking again.'

She spoke of God as if here were an equal, a familiar. She was brilliant and enchanting, but I felt very small being that close to such power. Mountbatten commanded the combined armed forces at that time but was playing with a remote-controlled model aircraft while we filmed Edwina. There were too many trees around their house at Romsey, so he dashed in, disrupting our interview, and made a call to close down a military airport for a few hours so he and a nephew could play with the model airplane on open ground. I had to remind myself that only a few years back he had been a penniless immigrant who had had the good fortune to marry a rich Jewess, and now he had monogrammed cigarettes.

Mountbatten had a boyish enthusiasm and no apparent doubts about his handling of Indian partition, which resulted in thousands of deaths, but Edwina was wise and she guided her impulsive husband deftly. I lacked the courage to ask about her relationship with Pandit Nehru, as she stubbed out another MofB.

Needing more information about Burma than I could gather in seven days, I crossed the border from Thailand, fording a river and spending some time with the Karens, one of Burma's ethnic minorities. Unlike the Buddhist Burmans, the Karens are Christians who believe they are the lost tribe of Israel. They had been fighting the Burmese army for forty years. I drank wine with their seventy-five-year-old general, who had never known peace. Every spring, as the Burmese mounted their annual campaign, he tried to defend the women from rape and the men from enslavement. His ragged, barefoot soldiers with their old rifles stood guard while we spoke. Half the Karen population had fled and was living in refugee camps in Thailand.

I made *Beyond Rangoon* in Malaysia, where we reconstructed not only the students' revolt, but other key moments, including the incident where Aung San Suu Kyi and her political followers were travelling to a rally, only to find the road blocked by soldiers. An officer told her to turn back, but instead she walked slowly forward. He warned her again. Still she walked towards the soldiers. After a third warning, he ordered the soldiers to fire. But her father was the liberator of their country; they could not shoot his beautiful, brave daughter. So she walked through them, endorsing her power.

When I was preparing and researching the film, I sent the script to Suu Kyi's husband, Michael Aris. He was enraged. 'You are proposing to impersonate my wife without seeking her or my approval?' I told him that I had sent him the script in order to seek his cooperation. He wanted nothing to do with it.

It was difficult to find an actress who could approximate Suu Kyi's grace, beauty and appearance. I had got to know David Byrne, of Talking Heads, and I recalled his wife, Adelle Lutz. She looked very much like Suu Kyi and had a delicacy and poise that matched well. I persuaded her to take the part. Through her, I came to know David better. His life, his every waking moment was devoted to art. He haunted every exhibition, saw every film and play. He had no small talk. At dinner he would write notes about a film he was making or break off to try out a tune on the piano. Adelle would conduct normal conversation, ignoring David's febrile imagination. This eccentricity followed him onto the stage, where his songs spoke to the absurdity of modern life. Adelle designed bizarre costumes for him to wear as he sang. They were her expressions of his multifaceted personality.

I cast Frances McDormand in a key role, and through her got to know her husband, Joel Coen. He and his brother, Ethan, made original and fascinating films. Whenever we met, Joel and I talked for hours. It was as though we had both accumulated ideas and questions about movie-making that we could exchange only with each other.

The Burmese government became aware of our plans to film in Malaysia and began to pressurise the Malaysian government. Tony Pratt, my production designer, built an enormous reclining Buddha in the Malaysian jungle. It caused anger and distress and demonstrations against us in this Muslim country, and a Malaysian actor was vilified for playing a Buddhist in the film. However, the Malays are not a belligerent people and it came to nothing.

Ironically, Patricia Arquette, who played the lead, was raised as a Muslim. More threatening was the Burmese government's assertion that allowing us to make this anti-Burmese film was a hostile act by a neighbouring country. The Malays apologised to the Burmese generals and assured them that they had given us two weeks' notice to leave the country. It was disastrous. We had only just started shooting and had eight more weeks to go. Our Malay lawyer counselled patience. As the two weeks came to an end, the lawyer approached the Malaysian government again. The minister responded by rescinding our permission to shoot in his country and giving us two weeks' notice to leave. As each fortnight came to an end, we would be given a further two weeks in which to leave – a triumph of diplomacy.

Patricia Arquette bravely tackled all the very physical scenes as her character is caught up in the student uprising, including some in which she had to get into a river. Here her courage failed her. Patricia had a horror of the leeches that abounded in the water. She would be close to hysteria as she pointed to one attached to my leg. One day, annoyed by her phobia, I said, 'Patricia, stop worrying about the leeches and start worrying about the crocodiles.' In the way that a greater pain will cause us to forget a lesser one, the leeches stopped bothering her.

I had also cast Spalding Gray, the master of the monologue, including *Swimming to Cambodia*. He insisted on swimming a long stretch of the river, challenging any crocodile to attack him. We watched from a bridge, and true to his boast the basking crocodiles showed no interest in him. Not long after making our film, he apparently committed suicide, so perhaps he was already tempting death to claim him and 'eaten by a crocodile' would have been a suitably bizarre demise.

He was staying in a cottage close to the river and told us of a monkey that was intent on attacking him. He explained that it could sense his highly developed sexuality and was worried that he would usurp him and seduce his mate. Spalding was firmly at the centre of his personal cosmos. He was cause and effect; the long evolution of humanity led inexorably to Spalding Gray. Despite his arrogance, he was fragile and tender. His plight – that of the hapless yet boastful iconoclast – was our own writ large.

In the midst of all these upheavals was the calm figure of Aung Ko, who played the monk who travels with Patricia in the movie. I met him during my researches. He had left Burma some years earlier but retained the qualities I found in many of the monks: a profound calm, an acceptance of whatever misfortune befell him, an absence of ego. Much as I admired these qualities, whenever I spent time with Aung Ko I had to fight off the urge to fall asleep. I tried to put him together with Spalding, but they cancelled each other out.

Burmese spies were everywhere, watching all our movements. I had a paranoid fear that they would plant heroin in my hotel room; in Malaysia the penalty for possession of the drug was death. However, we finished the shoot and got out of the country intact. There is always the fear of losing an actor or suffering the disasters that lie in wait for an action movie shot in distant lands. The river threatened in *Deliverance*, as did the malicious jungle in *The Emerald Forest*. Here it was the malice of the Burmese generals.

The Music

I returned to the room in Ardmore Studios in Ireland where I had shaped all my movies. I started to consider the music. I greatly admired the way Hans Zimmer entered a film and enriched it. I had got to know him early in his career, when he did some work for me. Back then he had a synthesiser that could provide sound and musical effects. He supplied the 'glue' that bound together the complex soundtrack of *Leo the Last*. His early work taught him how to conduct the dance with a director.

He had just made that great choral score for *The Lion King* and was at the peak of his powers. I apologised to him for my modest music budget. Up to that point, all my collaborations had relied on the composer sketching out themes on the piano, implemented – in the case of Ennio Morricone – with a range of instruments he could simulate with his voice. But when we got into the studio with the orchestra, it always sounded different from how I had imagined it, causing me to have tense discussions with the composer, who would then make hasty changes.

Hans had a computer with samples of every instrument. All film composers have this facility now, but he was leading this revolution. He could build the score and show the director exactly how it would sound. Changes could be made calmly and thoughtfully. When the score was complete, he would go into the studio and replace the samples with real instruments played by real musicians.

We sat at the computer keyboard together, with the film on a screen before us. We looked at the first scene that required music: the woman, the sadness of a lost child.

'What instrument do you hear?' asked Hans.

'Not strings – too mawkish,' I said tentatively.

'How about high woodwinds?' he suggested. He dialled up some samples and blended them. 'Now play me a few notes on the keyboard,' he said.

I hesitated. Hans was so relaxed and charming that eventually I dared. I tried a few combinations, and the woodwinds responded.

47

Hans picked it up and in his hands the theme emerged. This was how he entered the picture, and in this way we approached each scene. It was gentle and intimate and overcame the difficult moment when the director has to surrender a portion of the movie to another.

With some trepidation I invited Michael Aris to watch the finished film. He brought his younger son with him. Michael was moved by what he saw and apologised for his earlier antagonism. His son had been bitter about being abandoned by his mother, but seeing her as a heroine in a movie somehow helped him forgive her.

I finally met Aung San Suu Kyi when she came to Europe after being released from incarceration. She had seen our film in Burma. It had been smuggled in and covertly watched by many. The delicacy and compassion she had shown under such terrible pressure had left its mark on her face. She was a warrior, and I saw the steel under that lovely skin. Without her Burmese robes and the flower in her hair, wearing a tweed suit, she was revealed as very English. I understood why the generals saw her as alien. In marrying an Englishman, having English children and adapting wholly to the life of the wife of an Oxford don, she had, in a sense, abandoned Burma. When she returned to nurse her dying mother, her suffering countrymen reached out to her, the daughter of the father of their country, for help. How trivial her comfortable English life must have seemed compared to the anguish of her fatherland.

We were able to sit and talk freely because she had come to terms with the generals and her party had been allowed to take part in the election, which it won in a landslide. These concessions afforded the generals a degree of legitimacy, and the sanctions against them were lifted. To blunt her power, they slipped a clause into the constitution saying that no one who had foreign children could be president, so she rules through a surrogate. The generals also kept control of the army, and Suu Kyi is not allowed to comment on its activities. She is now a politician and must be politic. I hope that she is working for truth and justice behind the scenes.

When Suu Kyi elected to stay in Burma to help her suffering people, her husband, Michael, lost his wife and their two sons lost their mother. They were able to visit occasionally over the years, but when Michael was diagnosed with terminal cancer, the generals would not allow him or his sons to visit. They saw the situation as a means of finally ridding themselves of Suu Kyi. They would let her go to England to see Michael, but she would not be allowed back.

She had to choose between family and country. She chose to stay. Michael and Suu Kyi were devoted and deeply in love. How she must have suffered in that empty, guarded house, cut off from her ailing husband. The generals accused her of being manipulated by Michael. 'Little do they know,' he said to me, 'that I am her abject slave.'

I notice that the generals have swapped their military uniforms for traditional Burmese dress. I fear the change is cosmetic. They continue to brutally repress any uprising. Half the Karen population has fled to Thailand to escape murder, rape and enslavement, scarcely noticed by the West. Suu Kyi's struggle has hardened into dogma and she won't allow even genocide to deflect her from her programme of reform. We, her admirers and disciples, are devastated by her silence.

If someone had accused me at that time of being more concerned about Michael Aris's wife than my own, Christel, I would have had to agree.

CHRISTEL

In my memoir *Adventures of a Suburban Boy*, I described a concert I attended in 1952, when I was serving my two years of compulsory army service:

Beethoven's 'Pastoral' Symphony occupied the first half. As it followed its sublime path, seeming to rise like sap out of the earth of these very Malvern hills, I became aware of not one, but two girls. One was sitting to my right, the other on the row in front. The one in front was dark and slender. She could feel my eyes and half turned to reveal exactly the features I had divined from her back. I felt a shock of recognition. In some deep, dark place I knew that I knew her. I also felt a pull to the blonde on my right. I assessed her in my peripheral vision. Only two seats away, I was well within range of her sexual aura. The passage of the music exquisitely suspended the need to make a choice between these alluring possibilities.

At the interval we were offered coffee and biscuits and there was the explosive chatter that follows enforced silence. Everybody smoked in those days. I edged towards the dark girl, an exploratory excursion. She smoked intently, wholly involved in her cigarette. She seemed fragile, hugging herself as though to ward off the cold in that stifling room. She was both intensely familiar and deeply mysterious. She met my eyes for a moment, searchingly, as though I might have the answer to some urgent question. In that instant I saw a whole life spread out with her – passionate, musical, Mediterranean, melancholic, childless. She turned away as though warding off a blow. I felt the hand of fate on my shoulder, but whether it was impelling me forward into that imagined life or holding me back, I could not tell.

At that moment the sight line that joined us was fractured by the other girl as she stepped up with her friend to claim cups of coffee. It was a study in contrasts. Her green eyes swept the room, resting on me for a quick appraisal before skipping on to the next candidate. She laughed, open-mouthed, rat-a-tat. I glanced past her at the dark girl. She was watching us. When we took our seats for the second half of the concert, the dark girl's chair was vacant. I felt a sense of loss and desolation.

I reconstructed that scene in *Queen and Country*. The blonde was Christel. I discovered that her lover had left her. She was devastated and, of course, I came to the rescue. She was from a farm in north Germany. We married and had four children. She had a great, generous heart, and we had a passionate, contentious relationship. Someone described our marriage as the continuation of the Second World War by other means.

The children grew up and left home, leaving us exhausted from the embattled marriage. We began to drift apart.

It was then that a dark lady reappeared. I recognised her immediately. She had an air of intelligent remove. She was considered rather than impulsive; critical rather than embracing. She too was recovering from a broken love affair, as that first dark lady surely was. Irresistible. We were swept away to another life and a new beginning. My vulnerability to broken-hearted women probably stems from my role as a child in consoling my mother for the loss of her lover.

Another marriage, three more children – seven in all.

Beyond Rangoon was about a woman seeking solace in Burma after the loss of a child, and I was soon to lose a child myself.

TELSCHE

Telsche, our firstborn, walked at nine months and seemed bent on running away. It was a constant struggle to keep her safe.

We found her face down in the garden pond of the house we rented in the New Forest. She was not breathing; there was no pulse or heartbeat. I had glimpsed, but not read, a newspaper article about a new method of resuscitation: mouth to mouth. Somehow I dredged it out of my memory, and there was the illustration in front of my eyes. I blew into her mouth and, eventually, she started breathing. Sometimes in birthing there is a gap between the baby ceasing to be sustained by the mother and breathing by itself. Evolution came up with a solution, which is to seal in the brain's oxygen until the baby starts breathing. The brain is thus kept alive, while the rest of the body is apparently dead. This works for several minutes. My successful resuscitation of Telsche was written up by our doctor in *The Lancet*.

Telsche often said that she was born twice, once from her mother and once from her father. A special bond grew up between us. We co-wrote the script of *Where the Heart Is*, and she rehearsed the kids in *Hope and Glory* – their performances owed more to her than to me. She wrote scripts for French directors and won a posthumous César Award for the best screenplay of the year, for *Gazon maudit*.

She lived in Paris, marrying and later divorcing, and had a daughter, Daphne. When Telsche was diagnosed with ovarian cancer, she said, 'Dad, you decide what I should do.' I tortured her with poisonous chemotherapy.

Towards the end, we took turns sitting up with her all night as she endured the pain. In the dead of one night she said to me,

'There's no way back for me, is there, Dad?' I could find no words. Something cracked apart in me, and it has never come together again. I am patched up.

Near midnight on one of those dark days a doctor arrived, sent by a friend. He came on a motorbike, a tall man in black leathers. His speciality was pain management, and he had treated François Mitterrand in the last year of his life. He looked Telsche in the eye, and it was as though he connected directly with her pain, took it upon himself. He asked me how much morphine we were giving her. 'Pain eats morphine,' he said. 'What she is getting now would kill a healthy person, but she needs more.' In addition, he devised a concoction, fed to her via a drip, that ensured that during the last two weeks of her life she was free of pain and clear of head.

She died with grace. She said to Katrine, 'You have been a wonderful sister to me, and so have you, Daisy.'

'No, I haven't,' said Daisy.

'Don't argue with a dying woman,' said my loving, witty, beautiful daughter.

At her burial in the Cimetière de Montmartre, on a cold February day, I saw the doctor in his black leathers, standing discreetly at the back, tears in his eyes. He met her only twice. How could one who dealt daily with the pain of others feel such compassion for another? It was Valentine's Day.

What Remains?

A tomb in Montmartre,
Picked flowers dying for her sake,
Heather to remind her of our purple hills.
I resurrect them with a watering can.

A bonbon that she liked
Left by one who knew.

A cast-iron bridge flies above
The rotting sepulchres,
Roaring with urgent life.

I brush the grave as once
I brushed her angel hair,
Hair killed by chemicals,
The cruel, hopeless cure.

What remains?

She cannot taste the bonbon,
Or smell the flowers,
Or feel the rough softness of heather,
Or the coolness of water,
Or hear the clatter of life
On the bridge above.

What remains?

Fragments and shards of memory,
Scattered in my unruly mind.
I try to paste them together,
To make a whole,
To make her whole,
But they fall apart,
They drift away,
She is gone.

My second wife, Isabella, said, 'You died with her.' Her second child with me, Lee, was four weeks old when Telsche became sick. Isabella felt abandoned as I spent so much time with my first family. She was originally from South America, so living alone in Ireland was very foreign to her. In retrospect, I can see that this was a turning point for her. She could not rely on me for support. She started to plan her exit.

I visit Telsche's grave each year on the anniversary of her death, and afterwards take her friends and her daughter, Daphne, to dinner. We are happy and we laugh a lot, as she did. Because she was buried on St Valentine's Day, Paris is always seething with loving couples. 'Did love bring you to Paris on this day?' I am asked. 'Yes,' I reply.

Twenty years later, the sorrow has sunk down and embedded itself in my unconscious, where it marauds my nights.

DAPHNE WAS SEVEN when Telsche died. Katrine promised her sister on her deathbed that she would be a mother to Daphne, but her father, Lionel, married again and Daphne had to live uneasily with a stepmother. Lionel was tyrannical and frustrated all of Katrine's efforts to fulfil her promise. During those childhood years, Christel stayed in our little apartment in Paris so that Daphne had somewhere she could flee to when she needed to cry. Daphne's unhappiness eventually persuaded Lionel to let Katrine have her every summer. Telsche's great friend, Carole Bouquet, also nurtured the child. Carole had her stay one night a week at her home and indulged her. Daphne grew up either fiercely disciplined or wildly indulged. At eighteen she divorced her father and cleaved to her mother's family.

Somehow Daphne emerged as a warm, open woman. She fell in love with an English boy, Jamie. We monitored the relationship. He seemed able to tease her out of her dark moods and dance her back to joy.

Katrine arranged a magical Moroccan wedding, and Daphne asked me to conduct the service as a kind of secular priest. I wrote a customised ceremony for them, and the outdoor service was held within a curve of Grecian columns. As she walked down the aisle on the arms of my son, Charley, and Katrine's husband, Danny, she momentarily looked exactly like her mother. I was emotionally ambushed and wept.

When she became pregnant, the news filled me with joy. In July 2017 she gave birth to a boy, Leo. Daphne and Jamie brought Leo over to my house in Ireland and I baptised him in the lake at Luggala; my great-grandson. Even in a godless world, rituals are required.

Telsche's genes are in there somewhere, even a pinch of mine.

TWO NUDES BATHING

While I was editing *Beyond Rangoon*, I got a proposal from the American cable company Showtime. They asked several directors to make a film about a painting. I chose the anonymous, intriguing picture that hangs in the Louvre of two naked sisters sitting in a bathtub. One sister is delicately holding the other's nipple between her finger and thumb. It is of the Fontainebleau school of painting of the sixteenth century. No more is known of it.

I wrote a screenplay, inventing a story that would explain this strange pose. I suggested that the aristocratic father of the sisters has protected them from the ways of the world. Their mother, oppressed by her husband's coldness, has run off. He hires a portrait artist to paint his daughters, giving strict instructions that the painter must not speak to the girls. They, of course, ply him with questions about what they should expect from a husband.

Nervously, I sent the script to the appropriate curator at the Louvre. He replied saying my solution was as good as any other and that I should forge ahead. Thus encouraged, I started casting. Clearly, the breasts were very important to the story, yet I could not pluck up the courage to ask the auditioning actresses to take off their tops. It was too close to the cliché of the casting couch.

We shot the film in the Château de Brissac, near Angers, in the Loire. It was there that I discovered that the girl whose nipple was to be held had inverted nipples. There was nothing to hold on to. What was I to do? My make-up girl came up with a solution. She painted a shadow on the breast, as though it had been cast by the non-existent nipple, a *trompe l'oeil*. This worked in the wide shots, and for the close-ups we used a stand-in breast.

My son, Charley, was to play the artist who had come to paint the sisters. I asked John Hurt to play the strict, possessive father. I sent him the script but got no response. He was having a bad time. His marriage was collapsing, and he was staying with various friends and hard to contact. When I finally reached him, he apologised.

'I left the script somewhere, John. Lost it.'

'I'll send you another copy,' I said, 'but I need a quick answer.'

This was a thirty-minute film with a tiny budget, which we shot with a five-man crew. It was only three days' work for him.

John said, 'Don't worry, John. Of course I'll do it.'

I sent him another copy, together with a plane ticket to Paris and instructions about where to get the train for Angers.

Clutching the script and the plane ticket, he headed for the airport. Halfway there, he realised he had left his passport at Garech Browne's house, Luggala, where he had been staying. He raced back and retrieved it, but left the script and plane ticket behind.

At the airport he bought another ticket, made the plane by the skin of his teeth and, astonishingly, got on the right train for Angers, despite having been drinking heavily over the previous several days. He spoke to his fellow passengers in the train compartment and told them he was going to Angers, then fell asleep.

We waited on the platform at Angers to meet him. The train pulled in. People got off, people got on, but no sign of John. The train started to pull out. John's fellow passengers wondered if they should wake him. Didn't he say he was getting off at Angers? Someone shook him. With a roar, he leapt out of the moving train and fell in a heap on the platform, where he lay inert. His suitcase was flung out after him.

We took him to the château where we were staying, as well as shooting.

'Sorry, John,' he said. 'I was intending to learn the script on the journey, but . . .' He shrugged.

In the morning we dressed him in his heavy, elaborate, seventeenth-century costume, as he drank a beer to steady himself down. He asked me what dialogue he had in the first set-up. I said, 'Just these two lines.' He looked them over. We shot it and moved to the next set-up. He learnt the next speech as we lit the scene. I filled him in with the absolute minimum of story and emotion that he needed to know for each shot.

Thus we proceeded through the morning. He had not read the script, did not know the name of the character he was playing or even the name of the film. As we broke for lunch (a very liquid one in his case), he said, 'This is the way to make movies. All that rehearsal bullshit is a waste of time. Spontaneity is everything.'

Drinking steadily through those three days, John was wonderful. He was an old friend, and I loved him dearly. He played this possessive, authoritarian aristocrat out of some kind of actor's intuition that connected him to the period. The costume helped. Its weight and style defined the man.

After the three days, we poured him back onto the train.

The cable companies had their own honours at that time, the ACE Awards. John won Best Dramatic Actor for his performance, although he scarcely remembered being in the film at all. Nevertheless, he went out to Los Angeles and graciously accepted his prize.

There is a codicil to this story. Sometime later I published my memoir, *Adventures of a Suburban Boy*, and it was agreed that John would interview me about the book on the stage of the National Film Theatre, on the South Bank. As we were getting up onto the stage, he said to me, 'Sorry, John, I haven't had time to read it.'

'What are we going to do then?' I asked.

'We'll wing it,' he said insouciantly.

We took our seats, but John made no attempt to ask questions, and I felt compelled to dive in and fill the ghastly vacuum. What could I say? What I did was to tell the audience the story I have just written above. Afterwards I apologised to John. I said it was the only thing I could think of saying.

'Quite all right,' he said. 'It feeds the legend.'

Not long after this, he betrayed the legend himself by giving up smoking and drinking and settling down with a new wife, Anwen.

I wrote a stage play for John, *The Loves of My Life*, and we planned to put it on, but my friend of forty years died in January 2017. His voice, distilled from alcohol and Gauloises, a single malt of a voice, had caressed the nation for half a century. In *The Elephant Man*, it was *only* the voice. As Quentin Crisp in *The Naked Civil Servant* the voice swerved into a gay queenery. It could express pain and suffering as a monster exploded out of his chest in *Alien*. His Christ for Mel Brooks persuaded us that Jesus had such a voice. Its emollient tone spread over hundreds of movies, plays and commercials. On stage it put audiences into a light hypnosis.

We had a memorial for him at the magical Luggala valley, where we had spent many fine days together with our good friend Garech Browne. His two sons planted three Scots pines in his honour, in the presence of past and present wives and a long-time lover. I hope their leaves will whisper his name.

JOHN SHARED OUR DELIGHT in making *Two Nudes Bathing*. The cast and crew were so few that we could all eat at the same table each night. Ironically, the son of the Duc de Brissac and his wife played the servants. There was none of the crushing urgency that comes with a crew of a hundred and the servicing of a big cast. Normally, one never escapes the remorseless pressures of time and money, but here we did.

Digital cameras were beginning to appear at the time, but we chose to shoot with Seamus Deasy's Super 16mm film camera, with plastic fold-up tracks that Seamus could lay himself without the help of three or four grips. If we needed to get elevation, we would make a little wooden ramp and lay the tracks on top of it.

Digital cameras have got lighter and are becoming ever more sensitive to light, so that one can shoot in all kinds of conditions without lights. This has led to the ultra-low-budget film, and thence to the so-called no-budget film. However, what counts is not the camera but what you put in front of it: the subject matter, how you design the shots and tell the story and, yes, how you light it. The available light can be dingy – 'Nature is too green and poorly lit,' complained the painter François Boucher.

We blew our film up to 35mm and showed it on the huge screen at Cannes. It looked beautiful. However, it was carefully hand-printed and was not robust enough to allow for hundreds of copies.

Two Nudes Bathing was my only professional collaboration with Isabella. She managed this simple production single-handedly, and most effectively.

I DREAMT I WOKE UP

Seamus Deasy and I shot another film in this manner, this time for the BBC, for a series in which directors were invited to make a film about their own environment, about where and how they lived.

Hope and Glory, based on my childhood memories of the London Blitz, was my first foray into autobiography, and *Queen and Country*, about my army experiences as an eighteen-year-old conscript, is probably my last. These were films in which memory and imagination collaborated to create a fictional truth out of real events and people.

I Dreamt I Woke Up was more direct. I played myself as a film director tucked away in the Irish landscape I love. A female journalist, played by Janet McTeer, turns up to interview me and savagely accuses me of all the failings critics have levelled against me over the years. One never forgets the bad reviews, like *Time* magazine's dismissive one-line review: '*Point Blank* is a fog of a film.' Louis Mackerel of *Le Monde* apologised to me for his review of *Hell in the Pacific*. He said he was ill at the time and should never have written so harshly of it. He said it is a very bad film, but not as bad as he had said it was.

I put all their accusations together and wrote Janet an excoriating speech that cut me down to size. My responses to her criticisms were entirely self-justifying. For instance, she is scornful about my obsession with myth, until Merlin suddenly appears in the room. Later, she becomes the Lady of the Lake, emerging from the lake in Glendalough. Charley appears as the Green Man leaping out of a tree. A body preserved by the bog comes alive. It was tongue-in-cheek, but I wanted to externalise the spiritual, atavistic feelings we have about landscape, rivers, lakes.

The title refers to a recurring dream in which I would dream that I had woken up, and therefore it had the veracity of the waking world – a theme I later developed into a script, *Halfway House*.

I Dreamt I Woke Up opens as I dream of my own death and entombment. I performed the documentary elements myself, but when the film becomes mythic, dreamlike or transcendent, John Hurt becomes my alter ego. As the two realities collide, we eventually appear together side by side and converse – my practical, sceptical side arguing with my mythical, spiritual side, represented by John. I am sometimes asked how I reconcile my atheism with the spiritual elements in my films. Here I tried to address that. The film is an exercise in self-criticism, but it is also an attempt to address these contradictions. It saddens me that I will never work with John again.

Together with *Two Nudes Bathing*, this was the most pleasurable film to make. The satisfaction in making films comes not from the final product, but from the process – the intense relationships with actors and crew, the solving of problems, the emotional intensity. In the furnace of the moment, all thoughts of death are banished and we are temporally immortal.

Like most directors, I will work assiduously in post-production to make the film as perfect as possible, but once it is released, I seldom watch it again. There is much less pressure on these smaller films, but with feature films their high costs mean you are closely scrutinised all through production by the financiers and then tested by critics and the public, who can celebrate your film or reject it. A lot of people can lose a lot of money. We labour to make the film as good as it can be, then send it out and hope it connects.

When a film, made with love, is rejected, I always fall into a dark place of despair, overcome by a feeling of worthlessness. Failure is evident, but success is elusive. How do you measure it? Is it reviews, box office, word of mouth, a combination of these? There are always dissenters among critics. *Hope and Glory* had almost unanimously good notices, except for one, the very first that came out, *Variety*'s '*Hope and Glory* is not Art and not commercial.' My heart sank, and despite all the rave reviews and awards that followed, the niggle was always there: perhaps *Variety* was right.

THE HERETIC

David Lean said to me, 'We all have failures. Try not to make a famous failure.' My sequel to *The Exorcist* certainly was one. An audience expecting more shocks and gore understandably felt cheated by my offering. Objects were thrown at the screen, and people demanded their money back. The author of *The Exorcist*, William Peter Blatty, disowned it. Warners had pre-sold it, so were covered and in profit. The theatre owners had paid up and lost their shirts.

The head of the studio, John Calley, had asked me to direct *The Exorcist*. I read Blatty's book. As the father of daughters, I was horrified by it. To me, it was a story about torturing a child. I declined. The picture, directed by William Friedkin, was a runaway success.

Calley came back to me three years later with a two-page story written by William Goodhart. I was intrigued because it seemed to be not a sequel, but a response to *The Exorcist*. It was about goodness, rather than evil. I was tempted because I would be offered a large budget to make a fundamentally metaphysical film. I should have known better.

I recently received a letter which surprised me. It was from a man, David Kerridge, who wanted to make a documentary about *The Heretic*. He and his cinephile friends were great admirers of the film. He claimed that its enthusiasts were legion. He called and asked me about the making of the film. I told him how I had contacted my long-time collaborator, Rospo Pallenberg, and we sat down and wrote a script. It was fundamentally Manichaean, about how great goodness attracts evil to itself. Much later, I saw this happening in Burma, where the protesting pacifist monks were mown down by the generals.

I tempted veteran special-effects men out of retirement to help me with the locust swarms and the many difficult challenges *The Heretic* offered. I had all the resources of Hollywood at my disposal. I was able to get Ennio Morricone to do the score. At the time, at $14 million it was the most expensive film that Warner Bros. had ever made. It included some of the best work I have ever done, but I still find it painful to watch. The scorn and ridicule have clung to it.

I was so shocked by the failure that I lost my nerve for a couple of years, until I finally gathered up my courage and launched into *Excalibur*, which turned out to be even more difficult to make than *The Heretic*. Hitchcock said a successful film has many fathers, but a failure is an orphan. I am glad that two of my orphans, *Zardoz* and *The Heretic*, have gained foster-parents through their cult status.

ARDMORE

When I first came to Ardmore Studios in 1969 to do post-production on *Leo the Last*, I occupied a room that I was to come back to over and over again in order to fashion my movies. I cut *Deliverance* there; not only was it edited in that room, but all the sound effects – canoes scraping against rock, swirling water, paddles dipping into the river – were made in a tank in the dubbing theatre. *Zardoz* was next, a complex science-fiction story, on which many Irish technicians got their first jobs; then *The Heretic*, for which, besides the editing, we built and shot miniature sets on A Stage.

Excalibur was shot entirely in Ireland and all the post-production done at Ardmore. Tony Pratt's sets burst out of the confines of the soundstages. Holes were made in their walls to accommodate our ambitions.

The Emerald Forest, *Hope and Glory*, *Where the Heart Is*, *Beyond Rangoon*, *Two Nudes Bathing*, *I Dreamt I Woke Up*, *The General*, *The Tailor of Panama*, *In My Country*, *The Tiger's Tail* and *Queen and Country* – all found their shape in that little room over forty-five years.

THE GENERAL

Although I had made films *in* Ireland, I had not ventured to make a film *about* Ireland until *The General*.

Martin Cahill was a gangster. He was brought up in a sewer estate alongside the neglected, the forgotten, the unwanted. Their deprivation forged a fierce loyalty between them; it was a case of us against the world. Cahill was a talented thief, a master planner and the scourge of the police. It was not enough to plan and execute a brilliant heist; to complete his satisfaction he needed to make fools of the cops. If the pursuit got too hot, he could always retreat to the sewer estate – it was a no-go area for the police, where Cahill ruled inviolate. He harked back to the old Irish chieftains who rustled each other's cattle with reckless abandon and wit.

This was Brendan Gleeson's first lead role in a movie. A former schoolteacher and amateur actor, he astonished me by the way he inhabited the character. Brendan is a man of great goodness and wit, yet when roused capable of an alarming temper. Somehow his character mirrored Cahill's. They knew each other. In other circumstances, Cahill could have been an actor. Brendan's humanity would never have allowed him to be a gangster, and perhaps it was his innate goodness that shone through the cruelty and allowed the audience to love him. Hitchcock said Cary Grant was the only bad person who could successfully play good characters.

I made five movies with Brendan, and in each one he transformed himself. His method goes beyond impersonation. It is cannibalism. He eats those characters alive.

A leading actor in a film should become part of its inventions. Brendan quickly absorbed the techniques of the craft and became my collaborator. I cast Jon Voight as Cahill's police inspector nemesis. Our exacting work on *Deliverance* had cemented a relationship that would never be severed. He also passed on that experience to Brendan, and their scenes together soared as the two of them reached higher and higher levels.

The General had street scenes, and I cringed at red and blue cars and orange-garbed street workers distracting from the action. I opted to shoot in black and white. One could argue that film was at its purest when shot on that early, flammable, silver nitrate stock. When it caught fire, it produced oxygen, so it was almost impossible to put out. Safety film lacked the silky blacks and snowy whites and luminosity of silver nitrate. The colour stocks that followed were over-saturated and garish. The more film struggled to simulate reality, the further away it got. Film, at its best, offers a parallel, contiguous world as real and as unreal as a dreamscape. Film is metaphor.

Point Blank was my first colour film, and I struggled to deal with colour in a *noir* film that cried out for black and white. I decided to shoot each scene highlighting a single colour, moving through the spectrum from greys and blues up to the final scene in dark red. This unity gave power to the scenes. Too many colours drench the retina and dissipate the impact.

Although the river I chose as the setting for *Deliverance* was rugged and violent, the flora on its banks looked pretty and benign. I set out to desaturate the colour, which at that time involved painstaking work. These days digital grading allows us complete control over colour and density. At first cameramen were affronted by it, seeing it as a means by which their craft could be manipulated. Now they embrace it, with all its possibilities. As an example, a scene between dark-skinned and pale actors is almost impossible to light, especially if they are constantly moving. Philippe Rousselet devised a complex solution using a series of Chinese lanterns on poles that could be moved to follow the action and faded up or down as needed. In digital grading the light on the faces can be simply enhanced or dimmed for a seamless effect. Today, cameramen on high-end TV series, faced with having to shoot ten minutes of final footage a day, are instructed to shoot everything 'flat' – that is to say, without filters or artful lighting. The digital-grading technician becomes the artist.

Another innovation that dramatically changed film-making occurred in 1970, when Reeves Sound Studios in New York developed automatic dialogue replacement (ADR). Dialogue recorded in difficult circumstances needs to be replaced, which was formerly done by 'looping'. A sentence would be joined together in a loop of film, which would go round and round on the projector until the actor was able to synchronise to it. Then another loop was put up. ADR allowed the actor to work through a whole scene, which could be played back immediately to see how the performance matched from line to line to the original track, and to gauge the emotional effect. No dialogue recorded on the river in *Deliverance* was usable, so the actors were introduced to this new system. It became possible to review a whole performance. On every film since *Deliverance*, I have invited the leading actors to refine and improve their performances, often altering and adding lines. Because ADR stands behind us, we are released from the hushed solemnity that sound recording imposes. Fellini said, 'John, if the Americans find out about dubbing, we are finished.'

Like all good actors, Brendan embraced ADR and polished his performance considerably. When actors complain that the emotion of their voice in a scene cannot be reproduced with ADR, I point out that it is not their voice we are hearing but a mechanical reproduction of it recorded on iron oxide or digital noughts and ones. Film is a mechanical process, and we should embrace all its devices. I have never failed to convert an actor to ADR's efficacy.

The General saw me accused of glamorising a gangster. The film showed Cahill as ruthless and cruel and brutal, yet audiences loved him. I was alarmed when I saw this response in previews and recut the film to make him nastier still. It had the opposite effect. Audiences liked him even better. Brecht had the same problem with *Mother Courage*. Because of the money and effort it takes, a movie becomes, inevitably, a celebration of its subject.

The General was a success with audiences, although the accusations that I had glamorised a criminal continued, and despite my efforts to show Cahill's cruelty, I had to admit that the critics were right.

We are allowed to stare at the characters in a film. In life, we glance at people, then look away, unless we are in love. A curious phenomenon occurs as we watch a movie: we find ourselves identifying with the central character, however reprehensible they may be. We live through their adventures; vicariously we experience love and loss, tenderness and violence, commit deeds forbidden in life. Identifying with Martin Cahill disgusts us, yet it is irresistible. F. Scott Fitzgerald said, 'The movies have stolen our dreams. Of all betrayals, this is the worst.' We no longer have an original experience. We have been everywhere on film, experienced everything. Nothing comes new to us. We are second-hand people.

With the arrival of computer-generated imagery (CGI), film lost its innocence. Today, whenever people see a remarkable image, they dismiss it as made on the computer. At recent screenings of *Deliverance* or *Excalibur* cynical cries of 'That was CGI' have been aimed at movies made before that technique was invented.

JOHN CALLEY

The success of *The General* reminded Hollywood that I was still alive and had made a movie with what critics described as 'youthful exuberance'. John Calley called. He had been head of production at Warners when I made *Deliverance*. He was a beguiling character, with a modern mind, quick and witty, capable of absorbing a constant flow of information – books, movies, the stock market. He was much married and divorced and had no children. I was in his house one time when he was married to a lovely middle European woman who spoke only a smattering of English. Several of her relatives were installed. He found the Slavic language restful. He recommended marrying a woman with whom one did not share a language. He changed women nearly as often as he changed cars. I remember him leaning into Sydney Pollack's new Mercedes and saying, 'You must be very secure, Sydney, not to need leather seats.'

Calley loved women and automobiles. He also had a yacht, which he kept at the Marina del Rey in LA. I sailed with him one day, and when we were a couple of miles off the coast, he cut the engine and bade me listen. It was the drone of a million cars, the desolate moan of commuters, in some minor key unknown to music.

Calley was always anticipating Armageddon, and his boat was fitted out for survival. He monitored the news assiduously and his yacht was always on standby. He was afraid that he might be attacked by other boats less well provisioned than his. Because I lived in Ireland, he asked me if I could buy him a rocket launcher from the IRA.

He never wrote me a single note about my script for *Deliverance*. He worked in broad strokes. I doubt if he ever wrote anyone a note. He lived on the phone and by the phone. One day he called me after a meeting he'd had with Kevin McClory. McClory was an Irish boom operator who, to the chagrin of Cubby Broccoli, had managed to get the film rights to one of Ian Fleming's James Bond books. Broccoli paid him a fortune to recover the rights, but McClory then decided he had the right to remake it. Broccoli sued. It was especially contentious because McClory had lured Sean Connery back to play Bond, which threatened to embarrass the present incumbent in the series. I got a call from Sean. He reminded me that he had once asked me if I had ever met an honest lawyer. I said yes; Peter Bryan, my schoolmate, was a highly principled character. Sean believed that the distinguished law firm representing McClory and himself was untrustworthy, so he hired Peter to watch his own lawyers.

McClory was in Hollywood pitching the remake. Calley said to me, 'You should advise your friend Kevin that the budget for his Bond movie should either be more or less than he mentioned.' Because of his stutter and his Irish inability to pronounce 'th', when asked what it would cost, McClory said, 'D—, d—, dirty tr—, tree million.'

'It was something about dirty trees,' said Calley.

Nevertheless, McClory got the movie financed and made. Sean, who had said he would never make another Bond movie, did star in this one, appropriately called *Never Say Never Again*.

JAMES JOYCE'S PROJECTOR

Gerry Hanley, he who wrote the account of the Burmese campaign in the Second World War, was wandering the streets of Dublin during the 'Holy Hour' – three to four in the afternoon, when the pubs are closed. He had been drinking with the Shit Mackey, a poetic conman. Gerry spotted an ancient film projector in the window of a junk shop.

'That must have been like the projector James Joyce had in his cinema,' said Gerry, 'the first cinema in Ireland.'

The Shit's eyes lit up. 'What do you mean, "like" it? It is it, you fool.'

They decided to try to sell it to Kevin McClory, who had made a lot of money out of his Bond movie and had bought himself a grand house.

'We're pretty sure it is James Joyce's projector,' said the Shit to McClory, 'but we can't prove it. If we could, it would be worth a fortune, so you can have it for two hundred quid.'

McClory thought that was a bit steep. He examined the device and quickly found the initials 'JJ' scratched on it – the Shit's devious work, of course. McClory suddenly found the asking price just fine and pressed the money on the pair of them. He placed it prominently in his hallway so that visitors could read the inscription. The Shit told the story in every pub in Dublin and earned many a whiskey for his trouble. All McClory's friends, everyone, knew of the Shit's scam, except, of course, Kevin McClory.

Having read *Ulysses* on the third attempt, and inspired by McClory's projector, I picked the book up again. It is often said that the cinema was a huge influence on Joyce, but what films was he showing in his Volta cinema in 1909? It would have been the sentimentality and cruelty of Chaplin, the surrealism of Mack Sennett and the sadistic irony of Buster Keaton. It was hard to see what influence these films would have had on Joyce – the humour perhaps? If anything, *Ulysses* is doing what film cannot do: a stream of thought instead of a flow of images, the stasis of a single day instead of the urgency of action through time. Joyce was finding a form for the novel that film could not usurp.

Samuel Beckett, after watching *Battleship Potemkin*, wrote to Sergei Eisenstein asking to be his apprentice. We could have had an auteur as gloomy and wonderful as Ingmar Bergman.

Calley had seduced Stanley Kubrick over to Warners. Calley's combination of intelligence, wit and warmth was irresistible. You never imagined a studio head could be like this. However, whenever conflicts arose, he could never be found, although Kubrick could not be shaken off so easily.

It was being plagued by Kubrick's relentless attention to detail that finally forced Calley into retirement. The breaking point was reached when Kubrick invited him to London to see his new film, but when he arrived he was told he had to wait three days until his blood sugar had adjusted to the time zone before he was allowed to see the movie. He fled to an island off the coast of Maine. I wondered how long he could take the sensory and telephonic deprivation.

He was soon back as chairman of Sony Pictures. 'The Japanese revere old guys like us,' he said to me. 'Come and make a picture.'

John le Carré was another great man he had seduced, and Calley suggested I make *The Tailor of Panama*. He did his usual trick – he put us together and melted away.

I met David Cornwell (le Carré's real name) in his London flat. We drank champagne. He talked about Panama, but it was all in the book. He had moved on. He suggested that I write the screenplay.

I went out to Panama to take a look. It was le Carré territory all right – gangsters hiding out, money launderers, tax dodgers, kidnapping gangs, corruption, armed ex-Mossad guards protecting dubious bankers, and this wonderful canal with its flight of locks climbing the hills and another flight to get you down the other side. The locks require a great deal of water, so the Panamanians carefully preserve their rainforest, because when you cut it down, the rain stops.

I cast Geoffrey Rush as the tailor and Pierce Brosnan as the corrupt British spy who invents a political crisis and almost starts a war. Geoffrey had the fearless, brash confidence that Australians put on to compensate for being a long way away and overlooked. He had done every kind of part in every medium before he found international success. The opening scene finds him cutting and shaping a suit, all in one shot, a tour de force that proves his credentials as a tailor.

The facts were even more bizarre than le Carré's fiction. The Americans had an established garrison in Panama, but when they wanted to topple the notorious dictator Manuel Noriega, they had to invade a country they already occupied. The garrison was instructed to remain in barracks, while Navy Seals landed on the beaches, surprising diners in seaside restaurants. The object was to impose democracy by force, a policy pursued later in Iraq and Afghanistan with a similar lack of success.

We were warned about kidnapping gangs and advised to carry a few thousand dollars in cash to appease the smaller gangs who would take a hostage and demand payment within an hour, before the police could be called. If they didn't get the money right away, they would kill and dump the victim. Pierce was still playing Bond at the time, and although he was an obvious target, these small-time gangsters had all seen his destructive prowess on the screen and were nervous of tackling him. He would stride out from his trailer into the mean streets where we were filming, and the kidnappers would back off. At another level, the more professional gangs would take a victim and sell him over the border into Colombia, where the Farc rebels held hundreds of victims, financing their cause through ransoms.

In 1992 I served on the jury of the Cannes Film Festival. Gérard Depardieu was the president. The jury screenings were at 8 a.m., and as soon as the lights went down he would fall asleep and snore loudly. My job was to wake him up. Sometimes a jab with my elbow was sufficient, but on bad days it was necessary to punch or shake him. Jamie Lee Curtis was a fellow juror, and I loved her wit and originality. Several years later, when I was preparing *The Tailor of Panama*, I happened to be in New York when she was promoting one of her books for children at FAO Schwarz. She was swamped by mothers and children asking questions and pleading for autographs. I managed to get near the front and shouted over the din, 'Would you come to Panama with me to make a movie?'

Without hesitation she said, 'Sure.'

Unlike most actors, she did not wait in her trailer during the shoot. She preferred to stay on the set and be part of the process. She became a great friend and visited my home in Annamoe often.

My daughter, Lola, played her child in the film. Playing her brother, in his very first role, was the ten-year-old Daniel Radcliffe, a hasty replacement for the boy I had originally cast. Most children can act. Pretending, making things up, living wholly in the moment comes naturally to them, but not to Daniel. He was a sweet boy, anxious to please, but awkward. I coaxed him through the part. His good nature shone through. He was appealing. My daughter, Katrine, was at the premiere of the last Harry Potter movie. Daniel said to her, 'Haven't I been lucky? And all because of your father.' Had the producers consulted me, I would have had to admit to my doubts about his acting ability. Luckily, they did not. I had the pleasure of watching him grow into the role and learn his craft.

I took an Irish crew to Panama but persuaded Philippe Rousselet to light the film and Tommy Gormley to come as first assistant director. A Frenchman and a Scot – a perfect combination. Tommy has great organisational skills but also an emotional rapport with crew and extras. Extras are often treated like cattle, but they will do anything for Tommy. Philippe's subtle lighting is always at the service of the film's aims. We shot everything we could in Panama and for the interiors built sets back home at Ardmore Studios.

My son, Lee, had his fourth birthday on our arrival in Panama. He jumped into the deep end of a pool and sank. I pulled him out and asked him why he had done that. He said, 'Now I am four, I thought I would be able to swim.' Escaping the European winter for the sunshine of Panama, he was soon swimming like the fish that swarmed beyond the lovely deserted beaches. The air of menace that pervaded the country kept tourists at bay.

The tailor has invented a Savile Row history for himself and is haunted by his criminal uncle, Ben, a tailor in London's East End. I recalled that Harold Pinter's father had been an East End tailor, and so I asked him to play the part. On his first day, he sent word that he wished to see me in his dressing room. I found him studying the script. He was at his most self-important, addressing me in his pompous upper-class voice. I was dismayed. He was so far removed from the East End. He said, 'I would like to discuss a small textual matter. How would you feel if I inserted a comma here in this sentence?' I peered at his script. I said I thought that would be a great improvement. Could he ever find his father and the East End under the patinas of class and custom that now covered them? It put me in mind of a story told about Pinter. He wrote the occasional poem, which was often published in the *Observer*. When he composed a new one, it was his custom to send it to his coterie of friends and admirers. They were expected to call and congratulate him: 'Very moving, Harold,' 'I was deeply affected,' etc.

This poem referred to his love of cricket. It had but two lines:

> I saw Len Hutton in his prime,
> Another time, another time.

Harold became disturbed that his friend, the playwright Simon Gray, had not responded. As time passed, he became more and more agitated, and finally he called Simon.

'I sent you a poem, Simon. Did you receive it?'

Simon admitted that he had, but did not offer the effusive praise that Harold craved.

'Well, did you read it?' Harold demanded.

'I am only halfway through it,' said Simon.

Harold arrived for his first scene. The elegant playwright had metamorphosed into a small cockney Jewish tailor. He was brilliant. I remembered how his plays had influenced the dialogue style of *Point Blank* and how his screenplays for Joseph Losey had transformed the way serious films were made. Pinter's plays were disorientating; they threatened to undermine everything we depended upon, and *The Tailor of Panama* spoke of how our fragile world could be plunged into chaos by the fantasies of a self- serving man. The current occupant of the White House springs to mind.

IN MY COUNTRY

My friend Bob Chartoff knew of my interest in South Africa and the struggle against apartheid. He sent me a script based on a book by Antjie Krog, the Afrikaans poet. It concerned her experiences as a journalist covering the Truth and Reconciliation Commission's hearings about the shocking abuses inflicted on black South Africans. The framework allowed the victims to confront the perpetrators, who would not be prosecuted if they came forward and admitted their crimes. It was an attempt to purge hatred and revenge from the system.

At the heart of Antjie's story was a relationship between an African American journalist and a white Afrikaans woman. She identifies herself as African, while seeing him as an American. He cannot accept her as an African and is proud of his African ancestry. It was one of the ironies in this complex society.

In 1974, when apartheid was at its worst, I visited that blighted country with Charley, my eight-year-old son. It came about like this: Harold Pinter and other British playwrights had refused to allow their work to be staged in South Africa, as a protest against the system. I argued that while it was right to boycott sporting events and not drink their wine, art was fundamentally subversive and would hasten the collapse of this corrupt society. This dispute reached the British Council, and they asked me to go to South Africa. I laid down certain conditions: I should be allowed to visit the townships, such as Soweto, the universities and the Orange Free State, the heart of the Afrikaans people, and they must agree to a screening of my film *Leo the Last* to a mixed-race audience. I was confident that they would not countenance the screening since it involved a relationship between a white male and a black girl. To my astonishment, they agreed.

The screening was packed out. As the black girl gets into bed with Marcello Mastroianni, the audience gasped. They felt they were being given a glimpse into the greater world. As the mixed-race audience exited in a state of elation, the secret police were waiting to photograph those who had dared to break the apartheid law.

I refused an official tour of Soweto and instead went in after dark with a black arms dealer, whose profession guaranteed my safety. We toured the nightclubs, and I was required to dance 'the Bump' with two large ladies. Their big, high-slung backsides tossed me from one to the other, back and forth, to the delight of the onlookers, many of whom were so convulsed with laughter that they fell helplessly to the floor.

Soweto was the most populous town in Africa, but it could not be found on any map. The theory of apartheid was that the black and white races would develop separately; no whites were allowed to enter black areas, just as blacks were banned in white ones – except as servants.

I made friends with several white Afrikaners who were bravely fighting the system from within. They envied me my experiences in the townships and questioned me closely about what I had seen. The only environment where blacks and whites could meet and converse was in the universities. I met a young white student who was in love with a black girl on the campus. As soon as they stepped outside their university their union was illegal and they could not meet.

While I was there, Breyten Breytenbach, the Afrikaans poet whose fight against apartheid had led to his exile, returned secretly to his homeland. He called on friends and supporters as he moved across the country. He was covertly followed by the secret police and all his contacts were arrested and incarcerated, including a young lecturer I had met and was never to see again. I enquired of my government contacts as to his whereabouts but got no response.

Breyten was imprisoned and tortured. Some years later I was at a small dinner in Paris for William Golding given by Matthew Evans, the then chairman of the publishers Faber & Faber. Breyten, a pacifist and a Buddhist, was also a guest. Golding was very aggressive and accused Breyten of knowing nothing of war and suffering. Breyten said nothing of his torture and incarceration under apartheid and remained calm.

Matthew intervened. 'Shut up, William. You are behaving like a despicable bully. I am not sure I want to publish you any more.' Since Golding was one of Faber's big earners, my admiration for Matthew, already considerable, soared. Golding wrote Matthew a letter of apology.

One day, an Orange Free State farmer and movie buff flew me to his home in his light aircraft. He switched to automatic pilot and asked Charley if he would like to fly the plane. Charley took the controls. After twenty minutes, Charley said he couldn't keep the plane in the air any more, it was too difficult.

This farmer projected movies on a big screen for his black workers. They gathered outside on the grass and watched with no sound. We watched from inside the house, where the speakers were. I asked the farmer if I could speak to some of his workers. He said that none of them could speak English, which was why there was no point in putting a speaker outside. I found that several could. One gardener, who had daily contact in Afrikaans with the farmer, was literate and witty in English. I asked him why he never spoke English with the farmer. 'It would not fit into his view of us. We are bound to him. We are slaves. Better to act like slaves.'

The farmer and his family were decent people, yet they believed the 'Kaffirs' were barely superior to animals. The gardener knew that if he displayed his intelligence, it would challenge the farmer's belief system.

It seems that most people will simply go along with what is acceptable within their societies. An exception was Antjie Krog, a white Afrikaner who scandalised the burghers of the Orange Free State, where she was raised, and was driven out to Cape Town, where radical views were more tolerated.

Trevor Jones, who wrote the music for *Excalibur*, was a Cape Coloured. He won a scholarship to the Royal College of Music in London, but could not take it up because Cape Coloureds were not allowed passports, although they were given some privileges since they were seen as a step up from the blacks. They had some white blood and were mostly Muslims. Many of them looked down on the Kaffirs, and a sense of superiority towards them compensated for their inferiority to the whites.

Trevor appealed to the South African actress Janet Suzman, niece of the activist Helen Suzman, and she pressed the government to allow him a passport, which he eventually got. I met him just after he finished his studies. He was clearly highly talented, and I was lucky to get him. *Excalibur* launched him on a successful career as a film composer. How many talented coloureds and blacks were less fortunate and crushed by this cruel system?

I had persuaded Juliette Binoche to play Antjie, whom we re-named Anna in the film. I was impressed by the penetration of her research. When we came to each new scene, I noted that the previously blank left-hand side of her script was covered with her findings – how the scene related to Anna's life, its place in the drama, the emotional temperature, the narrative to be achieved and, finally, how it resonated with Juliette's own life. Opposite her, as the black American journalist, was Samuel L. Jackson, who was very much from the American acting tradition of responding to the moment within the paradigms of his personality. He was very smart and seldom allowed his personality to overwhelm the character, but bridled at my constraining him within my compositions. He complained that I did not give him the freedom to express himself.

One day I showed Juliette's script to Sam, and he was astonished. He said, 'My audience wants to see me playing a football manager or a con man or a journalist, but they also need to recognise that it is me. The character must not wipe out Samuel L. Jackson.'

This is the great mystery of movie stars, how they can play many different roles yet remain themselves, whereas actors like Jon Voight or Brendan Gleeson can transform themselves. Jon disappeared totally into the Irish police inspector he played in *The General*. On film there is something disturbing in these transformations. It makes us uneasy. We know Jon or Brendan is in there somewhere, but where? We would rather see Cary Grant or Sean Connery playing versions of themselves. I once asked Sean if he ever considered using a different accent in a role. After all, he won an Oscar for Best Supporting Actor for playing an Irish cop with a Scots accent. He said, 'If I didn't talk the way I talk, I wouldn't know who the fuck I am.'

The Truth and Reconciliation Commission travelled the country, allowing the victims of apartheid to confront their tormentors in the locations where the crimes had taken place. 'The truth will set us free,' was the mantra. A torrent of cruelty and suffering emerged. *In My Country* reconstructed that journey as Juliette and Sam covered it as journalists and gradually learnt to understand each other. The leader of the commission was Archbishop Desmond Tutu. It was important for me to meet him and get his blessing. However, when I got to South Africa, he was about to leave for the US, where he was to teach for a semester. His secretary told me a meeting was impossible since he was packing for his trip. I knew he was a cricket fan. South Africa were playing a Test match at home. I suggested to the secretary that he would be watching it on television. As a good Christian she could not deny it. I said, 'Ask him to give me the twenty minutes of the tea break at 3.40 p.m.' My request was granted.

Tutu was clearly wearied emotionally by the long, tragic hearings and anxious to be done with it all. He wished me luck, briefly, then we talked about cricket. Soon his broad grin and infectious laugh returned. On parting he said, 'Make sure you let God into the film, or else you'll come a cropper.'

I suppose we did come a cropper, though I blame myself rather than an absent God. The horrifying confrontations between the tortured victims and the police perpetrators made the relationship between the two journalists seem trivial. Brendan Gleeson played a notorious policeman who became addicted to killing. He would go out at night and pick off a Kaffir. He did it because it was acceptable, just as the ranchers who encroached on Indian lands in the Amazon felt free to shoot Indians. All of us divide the world into 'us and them' in various ways. It runs deep.

THE BREAK-UP

While I was making *In My Country*, Isabella stayed at home in Ireland with the children. In an attempt to revive our marriage, we had had another child, Lili Mae, an exquisite, magical creature who bound us back together, but this was only a temporary reprieve. When I got back from Africa, I found Isabella had developed a relationship with a neighbour, Adrian.

To soften the crisis in our relationship for the sake of the children, Isabella's first ploy was to assert that the journey to school was too taxing, and she asked that I rent her and the kids a house close to it. The children would only come home for weekends. Adrian became a frequent visitor to the house near the school, and the children got used to him being around.

I got a call from a newspaper to say they knew about Isabella's affair and would be running a story the next Sunday, and would I like to respond. I declined. I was concerned that when the children went to school on the Monday, their friends would have read the paper or heard about it. I sat them down and told them that their mother and Adrian loved each other and wanted to be together. Lola was twelve at the time. When I referred to the incident some years later, she claimed to have no memory of it. None of the children ever referred to the break-up. Lola told me that her mother never referred to it either. When Lola became resentful of this man being around, Isabella still offered no explanation. Finally, it was Adrian who spoke to Lola. He told her what I had told her: that he and Isabella loved each other and wanted to live together.

The children came up to me at weekends, and I would take them out to supper during the week. As time passed, Adrian set up home with Isabella and stepped into my role. They grew to like him. I became like a benevolent uncle, or even, because of my age – I was in my late sixties at the time – a much-loved grandfather. As the years went by, the children came up to my home less frequently. My son, Lee, came more than the girls. He had a great love of our land and shared my fascination with trees. I planted thousands of them over the years but also inherited some mighty old ones – great oaks and limes, California redwoods, larches, even a massive monkey puzzle tree – and one weekend, armed only with a coil of rope, Lee set himself the challenge of climbing the six tallest to their very tops. As his head crowned each tree, we all applauded and took pictures. For Christmas 2011, aged fourteen, he gave me a framed poem about a river, which hangs on my wall. The inscription reads: 'To my dear father, thank you for your passionate love of Nature which has helped guide me down a similar path.' There is one mighty oak that he cannot climb. The limbs are just too far apart. He salutes it, as it reminds him that Nature is unconquerable.

I took Lee to the Midnight Sun Film Festival in Finland, and we experienced that disorientating experience of the missing nights, as the sun never set. We bought the traditional wooden cups onto which your names could be burnt. Lee asked if he could have a second one with Adrian's name on it. Ruefully, I recalled how I had come to prefer my mother's lover, Herbert, to my father. Did my children experience the same guilt I felt?

Ireland was riding on the tiger's back, becoming the Celtic Tiger. The property bubble made us all millionaires, at least those of us who had houses. The world marvelled at the success of this little island, and many came to believe in the myth and borrowed the cheap money that the banks were throwing at us to buy property that would surely double in value in a year. We gained confidence, became cocky. This was not the sceptical, mordant, witty land I had come to love.

Nothing much seemed to be manufactured. Farmers sold land to developers and went off to live in Spain, but in the shadows was an underclass, people without property, people to whom the banks would not lend.

Leo the Last and *Zardoz* were both films about the rich getting richer and the poor getting poorer. I returned to the theme with *The Tiger's Tail*. A young Irish girl gets pregnant. She has identical twin boys. They are adopted by two families, one affluent, the other poor. I asked Sinéad Cusack to play the mother. Strangely, she got the script a few days after she rediscovered the son she gave away when she was very young.

One twin becomes a wealthy property developer with a trophy wife, the other a homeless man. The latter discovers his wealthy twin and tries to take over his life. They were both played brilliantly by Brendan Gleeson.

The property developer overreaches himself and threatens to bring a bank down with him. The film came out in 2008, before the bubble burst, and I was vilified for suggesting that it could all end in tears. Ireland was riding so high. How dare this

Englishman refuse to celebrate our success?

When it did fall apart, I was not praised for prescience. It was a case of 'kill the messenger'. On a radio programme I heard a presenter asking his audience if *The Tiger's Tail* was the worst film ever made.

The film did not do well, and I rather lost my nerve. Perhaps my career was coming to an end. I was seventy-five. I ducked out of the firing line and hid behind my laptop. As a kind of revenge, I dared to write and direct some radio plays satirising contemporary Ireland. I braced myself for further strictures, but none came. The radio audience is small, considered and tolerant. I was back in the fold.

During this fallow period, I wrote a theatre play, a children's book based on stories I had invented for my kids, and a novel about a group of people trying to make a movie. I published a memoir, *Adventures of a Suburban Boy*. I had film scripts I wanted to make, but not yet. Suffering from shell shock, I was not strong enough to go back into the trenches.

CINEMA HEROES

Taking a break, looking up from the myopia of my work, I realised that my cinematic heroes, the generation before me, were all gone. I had been lucky enough to meet and get to know them, as well as learn from them – Federico Fellini, Michelangelo Antonioni, Ingmar Bergman, Alain Resnais, Michael Powell, François Truffaut, Billy Wilder, Akira Kurosawa, David Lean.

While Lean was in the west of Ireland shooting *Ryan's Daughter* for MGM, I was at MGM's studios in Culver City preparing *Point Blank* with my two English comrades, Alex Jacobs and Bill Stair. Lean's blockbusters – *The Bridge on the River Kwai*, *Lawrence of Arabia* and *Doctor Zhivago* – had made him the darling of Hollywood. I was an unknown young English director.

Lee Marvin and I had been given a script which we both agreed was feeble, but I saw merit in the central character and wove a narrative around him with which Lee connected: a man left for dead comes back to life, determined to recover his share of a heist. It was a metaphor for Lee's brutalisation by the Pacific war and his attempt to recover his humanity through acting.

After long discussions, Lee finally agreed to do the film with me, on one condition. In what I would come to recognise as a signature Marvin gesture, he threw the script out of the window.

Under the influence of Pinter and Resnais, my English pals and I locked ourselves into the Bel Air Motel, off the San Diego Freeway, and fashioned our cryptic, existential script. Three weeks was not enough, but it was all the time we had. The screenplay I submitted was only seventy pages long.

I was summoned by the head of the studio, Richard O'Brien.

His desk was clear, except for my script, which looked very small and abandoned. O'Brien picked it up and thumped it down on his desk, trying to knock some sense into it. 'You'll have to explain this to me. This is not a script in any terms that MGM would recognise a script to be.'

He slapped it down again, chastising it. My mouth was dry. I found I could utter no words. He hammered the desk with the script once again. I could see myself on the plane back to London.

He stared at me with accusing eyes. A thought struck me that gave me some comfort: was he trying to be Irving Thalberg?

O'Brien's phone rang. 'I said no calls,' he barked at his secretary.

'It's David Lean,' she whispered, awestruck.

O'Brien stood up to attention to take the call. 'David, good to hear from you. How's the shoot going over there in Ireland?'

His tone was sycophantic. He smiled into the phone.

'You need another . . . how many extras, David? . . . Of course, David. Yes, David. Yes, David.'

He readily assented to whatever David required. He hung up the phone and sat down, still dreamily under David's spell. With a jolt of surprise he saw me sitting on the other side of his desk. He stared at me with incomprehension. I realised he did not know what I was doing there.

'Make a good one,' he said vaguely, with a wave of the hand.

The battered script had fallen to the floor. I reached down to retrieve it and backed out of the room. David Lean had saved my movie.

I took my battered script and shot *Point Blank* in eight weeks. David was still shooting. I edited my film, added music, did the sound mix and went back home to London. David was still shooting.

And two months later, when *Point Blank* opened in theatres, David was still shooting *Ryan's Daughter*. The Irish storms were not severe enough, so he shot one in South Africa. To keep him amused, MGM sent out copies of their new movies for him to watch, among them *Point Blank*. I was astonished to get a letter from the great man praising my film.

That was the beginning of our friendship, which lasted until his death. There was a strong connection between us. He started out as a film editor, as did I. We both came from the south London suburbs, he Croydon, I Carshalton. Neither of us went to university. We both had to struggle against the class divide. His family were Quakers, as were mine two generations back.

He began editing in the silent era. He cut on a Moviola, standing up. We discussed the importance of cutting with a certain pace and rhythm. He said that when the Talkies arrived, it became necessary to lace up a soundtrack alongside the picture on the Moviola. This slowed down the process, so David would memorise the dialogue of a sequence and then cut the picture without the dialogue track, recovering his essential pace. His early films were replete with this dynamic editing, the story thrust forward with ellipses and by the daring juxtaposition of images. His Dickens adaptations, which he also wrote, were a case in point. Stripping out the narrative from the beguiling descriptions, he released them from the captivity of Dickens's words.

After years of exile making his movies around the world, living out of the boot of his Rolls-Royce, he moved back to England and converted a warehouse in the London docks into a home. We had a number of conversations in that very masculine house. It was like being on a ship, and the view of the river fortified that illusion. He made an effort to connect with a new generation of film-makers.

He was nostalgic for the sense of community he enjoyed when he was making *Brief Encounter*, *Great Expectations* and *Oliver Twist*, that period just after the war when he, Michael Powell and Carol Reed were in their pomp, and Michael Balcon's Ealing was releasing its delirious comedies.

To coincide with his homecoming, the Cannes Film Festival mounted a lavish celebration of his career that included a dinner for five hundred and an orchestra playing music from his films. He asked me to make the address. We sat at the top table with Omar Sharif and David's fifth wife, whom he had met in Harrods the day after his fourth wife had left him. David was in a reflective mood and talked about the people he had known and worked with. His closest friend was Eddie Fowley, his long-time props man. He would send Eddie to find locations or solve a special-effects problem, like how to cover a house in snow and ice in the benign weather of Spain.

He then reflected on how the gypsy lifestyle of a film director played havoc with family life. He said, 'The tragedy of my life is that I always took the women who wanted me. I never had the courage to go after the women I wanted.'

'Does that apply to all five wives?' I said.

'Absolutely,' he replied morosely.

Omar said, 'Me too. I always took the ones who wanted me.'

I protested to Sharif that women swooned in his presence, that he surely could have any woman he wanted.

'It was the ones who didn't swoon I wanted,' he said.

David had been living for months in Bora Bora, writing his two-picture screenplay for *Mutiny on the Bounty* with his friend and long-time collaborator, Robert Bolt. I read the two scripts. The central characters – Captain Bligh, the rigid disciplinarian, and Mr Christian, the romantic – perfectly echoed the two sides of David's personality. What a pity these brilliant screenplays were never made as he imagined them.

It was there in Bora Bora that Bolt had a stroke that left his speech impaired. David told me how hurt he was that Bolt's son had said that Robert did not wish to see him.

I had been making *Hope and Glory* at the time. Sarah Miles was in the cast. She had told me how Bolt, who was her husband, was devastated that Lean had made no attempt to contact him after the stroke. He put this down to David's fear of his own mortality.

I told David of this misunderstanding. Apparently, Bolt had said to his son, 'I don't want David to see me like this – that is, felled by a stroke.'

The blood drained from David's face and he picked up the phone and called Bolt. They were reconciled, and Bolt went back to work on *Nostromo*, David's final project. Because David was then eighty, he asked me to act as the standby director the insurance company required. I read the script. Each scene was a polished gem. It was perfect, yet despite the epic scope of the story, it felt airless and claustrophobic. I once wrote that scripts should be badly written, rough sketches for a movie, not literary documents.

Yet however rigid his scripts might have been, Lean's films always threw up great performances. I asked Peter O'Toole what his experience of playing Lawrence was like. 'I was a galley slave,' he said. 'What got me through it was that I promised myself I would get my revenge on other directors for what David made me suffer.'

I once found myself sitting next to Alec Guinness at a dinner. I asked him how David directed actors. 'David is very interested in the externals of acting,' he said. I asked for an example. 'Well, he might say, "Turn your head to the left on that word."'

I understood this. He would want to cut on that word and he needed a 'hinge', as it was called in old Hollywood, a movement to make the cut viable. I have done this many times myself, but more deviously. I would tell the actor that on a certain word he would hear a noise and he should turn towards it.

Lean's epic period reached its apotheosis with *Lawrence* – marshalling armies of extras, huge sets, desert locations, daring action scenes, yet keeping the magic aloft, thrusting the story forward, making the characters come alive, all done with consummate skill. The famous shot of Omar Sharif emerging out of the distorting heat haze on a camel was a case in point. 'Everyone said you can't hold a shot that long. I wish I had not listened to them and had held it even longer.'

Although *Doctor Zhivago* and *Ryan's Daughter* were found to be bloated and increasingly old-fashioned by critics, his instincts and craftsmanship meant they remained immensely popular with audiences. He told me that he had been cheated by producers – particularly Sam Spiegel – and that *Zhivago* was the only film from which he had made substantial money. It was not an entirely happy picture. David was frustrated by the notoriously difficult Rod Steiger. Tom Courtenay told me that after the last day of the shoot, as he was leaving the hotel, David popped up from behind a sofa in the lobby to say goodbye. Tom asked him why he was hiding behind a sofa. 'Avoiding Rod Steiger,' he said.

He was garlanded with praise throughout his career, so when he was invited as guest of honour by the Critics Circle in New York, he expected to be celebrated further. He was devastated when Pauline Kael made a speech ripping his movies to shreds. His confidence was so shattered that it was years before he recovered it sufficiently to make what turned out to be his last movie, *A Passage to India*. It was not unlike my loss of nerve after *The Tiger's Tail*. Self-belief, even hubris, is vital when you shoulder one of these mighty enterprises.

He was only weeks away from shooting *Nostromo* when he was diagnosed with throat cancer. London was in the grip of winter, and I trekked through the snow to see him. His energy and enthusiasm were intact and he besieged me with questions. What did I think of such and such an actor? Who were the great young cinematographers?

I got a signal from the fifth wife, whom I had come to like and admire, that he was tiring. I stood up.

'Haven't we been lucky, John?' he said. 'They let us make movies.'

'They put every obstacle in our way to stop us,' I replied.

'Yes, but we fooled them.'

As I put on my coat to leave, he said, 'I do hope I'll get well enough to make *Nostromo*, John, because I feel I'm just beginning to get the hang of it.'

I knew what he meant. The feeling when starting a new picture that this time, now that I know how to do it, I can find the magic to lure the audience into the movie, to make them lose themselves in it.

All gone, that generation, but my own was also dropping around me. Ken Russell, Sydney Pollack, John Schlesinger . . . they were friends and colleagues. It made me think back to the greats I have encountered.

BRUSHES WITH GREAT DIRECTORS

Federico Fellini

I got to know Fellini through working with Marcello Mastroianni on *Leo the Last*. Marcello was his surrogate in *8½*. I love the scene where he says to the critic, 'I suppose you like films where nothing happens. Well, in my films everything happens' – a dig at Antonioni. Wonderful that such magnificent opposites could thrive at the same time in Italy.

Whenever I called Federico, he would answer the phone in a high-pitched voice, pretending to be the maid. '*Pronto.*'

'Is Signor Fellini there for John Boorman?'

He would drop his voice a couple of octaves and say, 'Ah, John, are you shooting?'

'No.'

'Nor am I. We are only half alive without a camera.'

8½ was a film about film-making, about Fellini's great attempt to transcend the limitations of the medium, to conquer his own doubts, his fear of not being able to hold it all together, to overcome the brutal logistics, the money problems, his own base passions, and to transmute it all into soaring spirit.

Akira Kurosawa

When I went to Tokyo to meet Toshiro Mifune, I was still struggling with the script of *Hell in the Pacific* and could not find an ending. I took the opportunity to seek out Kurosawa and told him the story: Mifune was to be a naval officer washed up on a tiny

Pacific island after his ship has been sunk in a naval battle. Lee Marvin, an American pilot shot down in the same battle, paddles his rubber dinghy onto the same uninhabited island. They fight the Second World War in miniature. They struggle, win, lose, advance, retreat, make a truce, break it, but I was struggling to find an ending. Did he have any ideas?

The master thought long and deeply. I waited patiently, expectantly. At last he spoke.

'They meet a girl.'

He saw my look of dismay, and suddenly his stern expression cracked open and he roared with laughter.

I met him once more many years later, when he came to London to promote his film *Ran*. We British directors gave him a dinner, and I was elected to make the valediction. It was hard to find a rhythm when I constantly had to stop to allow the translator to render my words into Japanese. Kurosawa's grim face and lack of response made it harder still. It reminded me of working with Mifune on *Hell in the Pacific*. Impulsively, I told the story of Mifune's translator, how he would beg me not to oblige him to translate criticism, and how Mifune would scream abuse at the translator while smiling pleasantly at me, as though I had nothing to do with the insults he was enduring. One day, I insisted that my angry response to his obdurate behaviour be translated. The translator said that to say such words to Mifune-san would be worse than death itself. I insisted. He knelt abjectly before Mifune and apologetically said my words. Mifune struck him in the face, rendering him prostrate in the sand of that Pacific island beach.

Kurosawa's face erupted. I recognised the phenomenon from my earlier encounter. He roared with laughter, then said in English, 'Impossible direct Mifune, only point him like a missile.'

Despite the agony, I still loved Mifune for his indelible performance in *The Seven Samurai*, one of the finest films ever made.

Michelangelo Antonioni

Antonioni came to dinner at my house in Ireland and we talked about the problem of pitching our movie ideas to financiers. He told the story of *L'Avventura*. Dino De Laurentiis called him and said, 'I hear you have a project. I'll send you a plane ticket. You come to Rome. You tell me the story. If I like it, we make it.'

Antonioni was famously laconic. He told Dino the story of a group of friends on an island. One of their number, Anna, disappears and they spend the rest of the movie unsuccessfully looking for her.

Dino said, 'So what happened to Anna?'

Antonioni shrugged. 'I don't know.'

'You wrote the script and you don't know what happened to Anna?'

Another shrug from Antonioni.

'Give me back the money for my plane ticket.'

I wonder if Dino ever saw the hypnotic cinematic masterpiece that was *L'Avventura*.

Antonioni's original style was about fixing the human figure precisely in a landscape, like butterflies pinned to a card. Jack Nicholson told me, after making *The Passenger*, that he believed he could build a performance within the narrow confines Antonioni allowed, but found he could not.

Antonioni wanted to make a film in Ireland. Anxious to help him, I asked what it was about.

'A yacht,' he said.

Like Dino, I waited for some elaboration, but none was forth-coming. I changed tack.

'Any thoughts about casting?'

He brightened up. 'I like Robert Shaw.'

Robert lived on the west coast of Ireland. I suggested that Antonioni and his producer should visit him while they were in Ireland. I called Robert and told him that Antonioni wanted him to play the lead in his next film. He was flattered but had prom-ised himself that he would not do another film until he finished writing his new play.

'But hell, I would love to meet him. Those great movies he makes. Why don't they drive over tomorrow morning and I will give them lunch?'

I said, 'That sounds just fine.'

'But, John,' he added, 'you know I am not drinking while I am writing, and I don't keep any alcohol in the house, so if they want wine with their lunch, they will have to bring it with them.'

I told them Robert was trying to stay sober while he wrote, so I gave them a couple of bottles and off they went.

Robert was so excited about their visit that he could not write all morning. When they arrived, he flung the door open.

'Come in,' he slurred, bottle in hand. 'What's this movie about?'

'A yacht,' said Antonioni.

'Sounds great,' said Robert, filling their glasses.

In the end, the film had a completely Italian cast.

Some years later, there was a screening of *L'Avventura* in the Roman arena above Taormina, not far from where it was shot. Under the stars, I sat next to Antonioni as he watched it with perplexed anxiety. He had lost his memory. He did not recognise it.

Robert also greatly admired Kubrick. Encountering him in a restaurant, he said, 'If you ever need me, I am yours.'

In due course, he received a copy of the script of *2001: A Space Odyssey*. He read it in a state of great excitement but was dismayed by the bland, technocratic nature of the two pilots. He told Kubrick that he would stand by his word, but he felt he was wrong for the part.

'Not the pilots,' said Kubrick. 'The first ape.'

Shaw did not think he was right for that either, but Kubrick persisted. He sent a letter to Shaw: 'I am enclosing a sketch of an Australopithecine man-ape. Without wishing to seem unappreciative of your rugged and handsome countenance, I must observe there appears to be an incredible resemblance.'

I don't know Shaw's response to that, but Kubrick finally had a ballet dancer play the role, in one of the greatest, most audacious films ever made.

Billy Wilder

Billy was the wittiest man I ever met. He was a fount of stories, and despite encountering him many times, he never repeated himself.

The last time we met was in Cannes. He had just finished what was to be his final movie, *Buddy, Buddy*. I asked him how it had turned out. He said, 'John, our movies are like our children. Every time you have a kid you hope he will grow up to be Einstein, but sometimes they turn out to be congenital idiots.'

He had a lot of Einsteins – *Sunset Boulevard, Some Like It Hot, The Apartment, Double Indemnity* and on and on.

Alfred Hitchcock

I was seated two places from the master at the dinner that followed the premiere of *Family Plot*. Hitchcock had arrived in a hearse. Jimmy Stewart gave a touching speech, and I detected tears in Hitchcock's eyes as Stewart spoke of his subtle way of directing actors. Hitchcock stood up to respond.

'I have often been quoted as saying that actors are cattle. I never said that.' He paused dramatically. Was he going soft in his old age? Was he about to recant?

'What I said was, actors are *like* cattle.'

Stewart laughed. In my mind's eye, I saw him again in *Rear Window*, under the spell of the master's manipulation of anxiety.

Michael Powell

I had long admired him from afar. I saw *The Life and Death of Colonel Blimp* at sixteen. I knew something was up when a movie could reach these heights, could have such ambition and scope.

I finally met him through Marty Scorsese. Michael had just married Thelma Schoonmaker, Scorsese's long-time editor. Michael had written a novel set in the Irish civil war and he wanted to make a film from it. Given our admiration of the man, Marty and I agreed to produce it. It soon became apparent that while Michael was happy to develop it, when it came to setting a start date or casting an actor he would shift his ground or change his mind. He was much the same age as I am now, so I understand the hesitation, knowing all the things that can go wrong, having lost the fearless ignorance of youth. He was pilloried over *Peeping Tom* and probably suffered a loss of nerve, as I have, I suppose. It was a gift to spend time with him and to talk about the mysteries of making movies.

Sergio Leone

I was in Rome working with Ennio Morricone on the music for *The Heretic*. I asked him to introduce me to Sergio, the man who had rescued the western from its decline into solemn concerns about reality and psychology. I was fascinated to discover how Sergio and Ennio worked together. It was all about finding the voice of the story, they said, the lonely vastness of the prairie, or the Spanish desert that stood in for it. That voice just emerged, plangent, haunting. It always said something about the loneliness of the plains. I believe they were rationalising to others what was instinctive to them.

One day, unannounced, Sergio turned up at my house in Ireland. He was making *A Fistful of Dynamite*, later retitled *Duck, You Sucker.* The James Coburn character came from Ireland, and Sergio was shooting a flashback. Would I help? He listed the locations and props he needed, and I was able to identify most – a thatched cottage, a donkey cart, etc. There were a couple I said I would have to ask about. 'When do you need to shoot?'

'Tomorrow,' said Sergio, with a shrug. It was the fag end of the picture, and he looked exhausted – the toll a movie takes on your life. I made him some strong coffee.

Sometime later I ran into James Coburn. He told me about his first day on the picture. He was costumed at the hotel, then a driver took him to somewhere in the desert. There was no sign of a film unit. Coburn was convinced the driver had taken him to the wrong location; the driver was convinced they were in the right place. A cloud of dust appeared on the horizon. Trucks and cars roared towards them. A camera was assembled. Sergio and his cameraman were screaming at each other in Italian. Sergio loosened

Coburn's jacket and rubbed dust into it. He moved Coburn's head from side to side, showing the movement to the cameraman. By now Coburn was getting angry, not even a *buongiorno*. 'When are we going to do the first shot?' he demanded.

'We just did it,' said Sergio. 'You look from side to side, confused then angry. You were brilliant.'

I saw Sergio's masterpiece *Once Upon a Time in America* on the opening night at the Cinerama Dome in LA. The story of Italian immigrants coming to America, it is a monumental achievement.

FRIENDS

There are friends with whom you can pick up where you left off, however long the lapse; there are those you never call but are glad to bump into; then there is the one you shadow all your life.

Robert Chartoff

Bob produced three of my films. He died almost fifty years to the day that we first met in the Soho office of Nat Cohen, for whose Anglo-Amalgamated film company I had just made my first film, *Catch Us If You Can*. In that half-century there was scarcely a week when we were not in touch.

Bob was a New Yorker. He took a law degree, then started an agency for Jewish comedians. He was a compulsive gambler, with a belief, like all gamblers, that he was lucky, born under a star. He had come to London on a gamblers' charter flight. As a side line he bought English movies and sold them to American distributors, which was how he came to be in Cohen's office. He sold Julie Christie's picture *Darling* to MGM, where his uncle was conveniently head of acquisitions.

The film had a naked Julie discreetly shot from behind as she walks away. MGM got cold feet. They told Bob that if he could release them from the deal, MGM would make him and his partner, Irwin Winkler, producers. Bob got a second fee by selling it on to Joe Levine, who did very well with it, especially when Christie won the Best Actress Oscar.

Bob found himself with an office in the Irving Thalberg building at MGM, a producer with no projects. MGM gave him the latest

Elvis Presley movie to produce, but it was already under way and Elvis's manager, Colonel Tom Parker, was effectively the producer.

I was in LA doing research for my BBC documentary about D. W. Griffith. I called in on Bob in his splendid new office, and he took me onto the set to meet Elvis. I talked with him in his plush trailer. Elvis had seen the Beatles' films and mine with the Dave Clark Five, retitled in the US as *Having a Wild Weekend*. He recognised that his movies were bland and he wanted to be more daring, but he was afraid of upsetting the Colonel and MGM. He seemed embarrassed to be Elvis Presley. There was nothing in his character to connect him with the brilliant performer. He behaved like an imposter. Very tentatively, he wondered if I would be interested in working with him.

He took me to see his new tour bus, of which he was very proud. He pointed out the bed, the sofas and the bar. Gold paint figured strongly.

Back in his office, Bob introduced me to Judd Bernard. He was a PR guy who wanted to be a producer. He had a bunch of scripts that he had borrowed, stolen or optioned, but no producer deal. Bob and Irwin had no projects and weren't sure how to get them. It seemed a natural fit. Judd was fast-talking and overbearing. He trashed current movies and movie stars. He cast them in imaginary films and improvised the scathing reviews they would get. He had the answers and was wittily opinionated. He pressed a script into my hands and asked me my waist measurement. He then pressed a pair of pants into my arms, for which he charged me twenty dollars. He could not face up to what his waistline had become and had bought pants that would have fitted the man he used to be. I was face to face with Sammy Glick, straight out of Budd Schulberg's book *What Makes Sammy Run?* The script was awful.

I talked with Bob and found his views on film and life reassuringly sympathetic after the apocalyptic brashness of Judd.

It was Judd who sent me another bad script. He also sent it to Lee Marvin, who was shooting *The Dirty Dozen* in London. Lee didn't like the script either, but he liked what I wanted to do with it. As I related earlier, he said, 'I'll make this flick with you, on one condition,' and threw it out of the window. We rewrote it from top to bottom.

When I got to MGM, I found I had three producers: Bob, Irwin and Judd. Bob was helpful and subtle; the other two had opinions and interfered. I was prickly and defensive, and told them I would talk only to Bob. The film was *Point Blank*, and it was a great success. It launched all three of them as producers and my career as a director.

Bob once sent me a script called *Rocky* and asked me to direct it. I found it ridiculously sentimental and urged him not to produce it. He framed my letter and hung it on his wall. He made a fortune out of the *Rocky* movies.

As a gambler he believed implicitly in his good luck, and I witnessed some of his spectacular wins. He never spoke about his losses. With the *Rocky* movies, good luck became good fortune, and he always gave thanks for it with his legendary generosity. He helped so many people, emotionally, spiritually and financially. And it was always spontaneous. In a café in India, he was impressed by two bright boys of eight and ten who were already working full-time as waiters. The boys' impoverished father had sold them to the café's owner. Bob bought them back. He found a teacher, gave him money, told him to instruct them in English and said, 'I will be back next year to see how they're doing.' That grew into three schools and seven hundred students, funded and supported by Bob in the poorest part of India.

We played tennis together all those years and our friendship even survived his nasty, sneaky spin shots. His shoulder and my feet finally brought an end to a fierce forty-year rivalry, in which neither of us really cared who won.

We did other films together and many more separately, but I always sent him my scripts for his comments, and he sent me his for mine. Whenever we read a great book, we would send it to each other, so we had a literary brotherhood nurtured through that half-century. We travelled our paths in parallel. Because we were so close, people remarked on how much we resembled each other. Were we brothers? they asked. 'More or less,' we would reply.

We comforted each other over our failing marriages and followed the fortunes of each other's many offspring. He had had a Jewish mother who constantly complained, and his role as a child was to charm and placate her, then melt out of her way. He applied the same treatment to his first two wives – charm, placate, melt away. It drove them both crazy. When they needed him, he was not there.

Tom Wolfe was a mutual friend. On my way to LA, I stopped off to see him in New York. His book *The Right Stuff* was about to come out. I read it on the plane to LA and then gave it to Bob. He bought the film rights and made a wonderful film of it. There was a girl working on the picture whom he fell for. Her name was Jennifer Weyman, and she was attractive, delicate, intelligent. He wooed her assiduously and patiently, but she resisted.

He was alone. I was staying with him in his Malibu beach house. I was drying myself after an ocean swim and asked him where I should put the towel. 'Drop it anywhere,' he said. 'There's no woman in this house.'

Jenny eventually succumbed. I was saddened at their wedding

because I felt she did not love him. She looked scared. His love for her had somehow compromised her. Even so, later on I was impressed by the way he cared for her but encouraged her to pursue her interests. Instead of melting away, he was always there for her. Something extraordinary happened: I saw her gradually falling in love with him. That love expanded and deepened, and they were together for twenty-five years.

Bob called me one day to say he had pancreatic cancer and had only three or four weeks to live. He was resolved. 'I have had a great life,' he said. 'We all have to go sometime.' But Jenny fought to keep him. She found a new experimental treatment, and he survived another two years.

He made the long journey to Ireland and stayed with me for a week. India had been a big influence on him, as had Buddhism. Watching his marriage to Jenny mature, I realised that the gambler was gone. He had acquired wisdom, and I started to feel a bit lightweight in his presence. Under his eye, Jenny burgeoned. He became reconciled to Phyllis, his first wife, and nursed his errant children back to equilibrium. He was enlightened.

Before he got ill, I persuaded him to accompany me on my annual pilgrimage to the Skelligs. The island of Skellig Michael is a finger of rock jutting out of the sea six miles off the coast of Kerry, in the south-west of Ireland. At its pinnacle are the beehive huts that housed the monks who lived there. Vertiginous steps cut from the rock lead the way to them. A fishing boat will take you to the Skelligs, but if the wind is unfavourable, you may not land. Now that my feet betray me, I no longer make my annual trip.

The Skelligs were closed to the public some years back to allow archaeologists to excavate. I got permission to visit and saw how under the huts, at a deeper, pre-Christian level, there were snake carvings. Could it be that Patrick cast out not the snakes, but the snake worshippers? Bob and I stood at the summit of Skellig Michael, both of us moved by its spiritual aspirations, reaching up to heaven. Bob experienced an epiphany on that rock, an awareness of his own spirit, a confirmation of his eternal soul. I argued that we have no soul or centre, that we are defined only by how we respond to the external world. The Skelligs or Mozart's *Requiem* or a beautiful landscape are metaphors for the absent soul. We become a construct of metaphors welded together by the love we give and receive. Bob shook his head and smiled. He knew. He believed. His many trips to India had brought him close to Buddhism and he meditated every day. He connected directly with the spirituality of the Skelligs. He would have none of my metaphors. His calm conviction irritated me, or perhaps I envied him. I asked Bob where this inner spirit resided. Was it in his brain, his heart or his gut? Did he talk to it? Does it respond? He regarded me pityingly.

'It just is. A calmness, a stillness.'

'That sounds like death,' I responded.

'On the contrary,' he said, 'it is about becoming fully alive.'

'There is no within,' I insisted, 'only other people and the wonder of the outer world. The spirit is a delusion.'

'Why do you come here every year?' he asked me.

Many of those he had helped were at his memorial service. I always thought I was his best friend, but many of the people there thought they were as well. As I spoke, I felt a wave coming up from those two hundred people. It was Bob's love, and it washed over us and embraced us all.

At the end, Bob and I both needed to walk with a stick. In his dying days he asked Jenny to bequeath his to me. I take it out for a walk now and then and talk to Bob as I used to do.

CAMERAMEN

The unsung heroes of movie-making are the cameramen. They come from different backgrounds and nationalities but share the language of light.

Vilmos Zsigmond, the cameraman on *Deliverance*, was a film student in Budapest in 1956, when Russian tanks crushed the freedom movement in Hungary. Vilmos and his fellow student, László Kovács, grabbed cameras and filmed it all – young men clambering onto the tanks with Molotov cocktails, protesters being gunned down in the streets. Dodging bullets, they fled to the Austrian border with the film. Theirs was the only footage of the brutal Russian repression, and it was eagerly sought after by TV news. Money was pressed upon them. They said, 'We don't want money, we want to be cameramen in America.'

Promises were made and broken, and the two boys eventually found jobs doing the night shift in film labs. The cameramen's guild would not accept them as members, so they worked on low-budget, non-union movies. It was obvious that Vilmos was a great talent, and I was able to employ him because we shot *Deliverance* in a non-union state. As a non-member, his remarkable work on the picture was not rewarded by the members of the American Society of Cinematographers, but it did persuade Steven Spielberg to hire him for *Close Encounters of the Third Kind*, for which he won an Oscar.

Vilmos was one of the first cameramen to come out of a film school. Traditionally, cameramen serve an apprenticeship. They start out as clapper-loaders, doing exactly that – operating the clapperboard that records the scene numbers and synchronises sound and picture. They load the film into the camera, can and tape up the exposed film, and send it to the laboratory for processing. They gather experience and eventually move up to focus-puller – the skilled job of keeping the action in focus, working closely with the operator. The next step up is to camera operator, where they watch the director of photography at close quarters, finally aspiring to his or her role.

This apprentice system means that cameramen are in a direct line to the very beginnings of film-making. Skills and knowledge are learnt and, like a baton, passed on.

I prefer a DP who also operates, which makes the collaboration more intimate, but sometimes, when heavy lighting is required, it is necessary to split the jobs. A DP will also have on his team a gaffer, who is in charge of setting the lamps, and a key grip, who lays down the tracks and figures out how to manipulate the camera into the movements the director requires.

The DP is at the centre of the process, and I have learnt so much from the ones with whom I have worked. Phil Lathrop, the DP on *Point Blank*, had been a great operator on movies like Orson Welles's *Touch of Evil*. Right at the beginning Phil said, 'Whatever shot you want, John, I'll make it work.' The more difficult the set-up, the more he was stimulated. He was dapper and neat and always wore a jacket and tie. When faced with a difficult set-up, he would light up his pipe and puff away. Everyone smoked in those days, and sometimes a take would be spoilt as smoke drifted into the shot.

For *Hell in the Pacific*, I was fortunate enough to get the great Conrad Hall. His father was the co-author of *Mutiny on the Bounty*, and Conrad was born in Tahiti. He knew all about that treacherous tropical light. He loved movie-making and his enthusiasm pulled the crew with him. He had worked with Richard Brooks on movies such as *In Cold Blood* and learnt much from him that he passed on to me. For instance, once a good take has been achieved, move immediately to the next set-up and don't waste time congratulating each other or taking a break. Conrad also taught me to keep black spray paint handy to dull off intrusive high lights, which is much quicker than setting a flag to shield the light. He took his time when lighting, so was clever enough to have a gaffer who moved fast in setting the lights. He also had a key grip, Art Brooker, whose ingenuity took gripping to a new level. Apart from lightning speed in laying down tracks, Art found ways of setting the camera in awkward places, by digging out trenches or suspending it from ropes, while always making sure it allowed the operator to move freely.

As I realised the problems I would face in making *Deliverance*, I kept thinking not of the DP, but the key grip. I called Art and discussed the challenge facing me in the river: the need to set the camera low in the water yet anchor it securely to the riverbed so that the operator can pan with the action. Art, as I expected, was ready with solutions. He was a tall, powerful, handsome man. Even though he had been brought up in an orphanage and never knew his mother, he loved the company of women and was always at ease with them, and they loved his grace and charm.

My thoughts turned to Conrad Hall as DP on *Deliverance*. He was heroic in making *Hell in the Pacific*. After that film he went on to make *Butch Cassidy and the Sundance Kid*. His lyrical work on that picture cemented his reputation, but he declared that he had decided to direct and would no longer work as a DP.

I had met Vilmos and seen his work. He was tough and wiry and hungry. He liked to operate as well as light, which was important on this picture, for many of the difficult river scenes would be shot by just the three of us: Vilmos, me and Art.

'Who is Art Brooker?' Vilmos asked.

'Your key grip,' I replied.

He said he had his own grip and that it was his prerogative to choose his crew. I told him how important Art was to the picture and that I had already hired him.

They clashed at first once filming started, but Vilmos was soon converted as he saw Art devise ways of achieving impossible shots.

Vilmos was very adept at panning the canoes through the rapids on telephoto lenses. In rehearsal he would mark focus points by a tree or bush on the far bank, and the actors never had to repeat a take because of a loss of focus. He curled himself round that camera like a monkey, and Art would have to peel him off to take it to the next set-up. After *Deliverance*, Vilmos took Art on every picture he did.

It is as important to cast the cameraman as it is to cast the actors. My next film was *Zardoz*, a science-fiction fantasy, and I wanted Geoffrey Unsworth as DP. Geoffrey was an old magician with a twinkling eye. He always looked perplexed when he came onto the set. Had he wandered onto the wrong stage? He would glance around in puzzlement, while his devoted crew would study his expression uneasily, trying to fathom his mood. He would survey the proffered faces. 'Just tell us what we have done wrong, Geoffrey,' they would plead mutely. And he would look back, his eyes wrinkled in gentle mockery, as though to say, 'You're teasing me.' Then they would remember, a task omitted, and scurry off to rectify it.

Only his operator, Peter MacDonald, would stand aloof, head averted from this pantomime. He knew that when the great illusionist was casting spells, the sole defence was to avert your eyes. Without speaking a word, Geoffrey had exerted total control. Only now would he convey his wishes, in a husky whisper that all strained to catch.

When the actors arrived, he included them in his aura of serene confidence and benign affection. They felt safe in Geoffrey's hands, and actresses adored him as he caressed them with light, their anxieties evaporating in his presence. Daddy would take care of them. Behind those dusty, smeary glasses a child's eyes looked out, smiling in wonderment, extending an invitation: 'Look at this place of make-believe and delight. Come in and play.'

Yet under this facade, and despite all the years and all the movies – *2001*, *Cabaret* – he was racked with anxiety every day at rushes, because he was continuously taking risks, he lit on the edge, pressing for perfection. It was this that fed him too, gave him his inexhaustible passion for his craft.

He was gracious and softly spoken. Where many DPs bellow at their electricians, Geoffrey would say, 'Would you mind putting a barn door on that 2k light?' and then thank the sparks for doing so. The set was quiet as his crew strained to hear his whispered instructions.

Apart from our detailed planning in pre-production, Geoffrey and I hardly spoke during the *Zardoz* shoot. When I inspected a set he had lit, Geoffrey would watch my reactions. If I examined the light on an actor's face, he would have a filter put on the key light. Geoffrey would not have lasted a day on the river for *Deliverance*, nor would Vilmos have been able to weave Geoffrey's magic on *Zardoz*.

Eastman Kodak colour film was, and is, over-saturated, and DPs and directors have always strived to find ways of softening or de-saturating this lurid stock. 'Flashing' was tried for a while. This involved exposing the film to light for a moment before loading it in the camera. This made the colours less assertive, but it was hit or miss and difficult to get right.

When colour first came in, DPs continued to light as they did for black and white, separating the different planes and objects by back or side light. The set of a black-and-white film would typically be lit by many lamps and have multiple flags and gobos to cut the light off from where it was not required. Applied to colour film, this direct light looked harsh and lurid.

Geoffrey and a few other DPs began to use indirect light. Lamps were trained on panels of white polystyrene, giving a reflected overall light that softened the harsh colours. At a crude level this made lighting much easier, but it was fundamentally dull and anodyne. Geoffrey refined the method. He used a fog filter in the camera, smoke to diffuse the light and shot with the lens wide open – all devices to diffuse the colours and give an effect close to the late Turner paintings. This required a delicate balance, particularly in matching the diffusion from shot to shot so that they would cut together smoothly. Other DPs copied Geoffrey, but most gave up. It was too difficult.

A few films were made in this style between 1975 and 1979, but then the studios banned it. When these delicate negatives were submitted to high-speed printing, they fell apart. The prints looked murky and out of focus. This was the period when movie marketing in the US changed. Films began to open with four thousand prints, bolstered by heavy advertising aimed at getting most of their money back in the first weekend. High-speed printing became the norm, and it required strong, sharp negatives.

In *Zardoz*, an elite lived in a perfectly protected bucolic environment, and Geoffrey gave it a lovely pastel look. In contrast, the rest of humanity lived in the harsh Outlands, which required a bleak, sharp look. The film was not successful, so it was not submitted to high-speed printing. Over the years the colours faded, and my own print no longer has the beautiful luminosity that Geoffrey gave it.

Recently, 20th Century Fox informed me that they wanted to restore the film, and would I help? They intended to re-release it. I asked why they were doing this to a failed movie. They replied that after forty years there was a continued and growing interest in it. I knew it had its admirers, many of them fanatical. Watching it, said its fans, was a spiritual experience. It seems the film had gone from failure to classic, without ever passing through success.

I went over to 20th Century Fox in LA and tried to bring *Zardoz* back to its original condition. Geoffrey had died many years before. As a tribute to him, I wanted audiences to see the magic he had achieved.

All these concerns about colour have disappeared with the advent of digital grading. Film is now obsolete. Most new movies are shot on digital cameras and projected in cinemas on digital projectors. Digital grading gives the DP and director complete control of colour and density. Dirt and scratches on the screen are a thing of the past.

Geoffrey's wonderful operator, Peter MacDonald, was a master of fluid movement. Where Geoffrey was vague and mild, Peter was focused and tetchy. The two of them constantly bickered in their quest for perfection. A camera operator has two handles: one that controls movement to left or right and another that deals with up and down. Between them they can achieve whatever movement is required. Some operators never master the handles and rely on the less delicate pan handles, but Peter was so adroit with them that he had a party trick whereby he taped a pen to the lens and wrote his signature on a piece of paper.

I had planned to have Geoffrey light *Excalibur* for me. Sadly, he died before we started shooting. Peter suggested Alex Thomson. Alex had been fired from *Jesus Christ Superstar*. The film had not been going well, and Alex unfairly took the rap. His reputation was ruined and he never got to shoot another picture. However, Geoffrey had hired him to do second unit on several of his films, and he was able to simulate Geoffrey's methods.

I told Alex that I wanted a magical, luminous effect, and he came up with several ideas, two of which I enthusiastically accepted. He put a 'spot' filter in the back of the lenses. Dotted with tiny black spots, it produces a kind of antique effect. His other idea was brilliant: he suggested projecting strong green light on the mosses and leaves to produce a luminous effect throughout the exterior wooded scenes. He was a tower of strength. We did all the special effects in camera. Nothing was added in post-production. Alex was nominated for an Oscar for his work on *Excalibur*, and he went on to do fine work on many movies.

This was one of the last movies before CGI and digital grading, and it had a mono soundtrack. I made a stereo mix, but when I previewed in the US the outer speakers were often muffled by the curtains, making the music and sound effects less present.

THE EMERALD FOREST WAS SET in the Amazon. As part of my research, I lived with an Amerindian tribe in the Xingu area of the rainforest and travelled extensively through that vast, dense region.

Back in Europe, I pondered the problems – heat and humidity, snakes, mosquitoes, disease, and the fact that the high canopy of trees meant that at ground level the forest was very dark, with very little sunlight percolating through. The glory of the rainforest is up there in the canopy; at ground level it is a shabby, tangled place.

I had become aware of the work of French cameraman Philippe Rousselet. I loved the subtle light he achieved. I talked to him about these problems. Would he withstand the conditions and pressure of shooting in the rainforest? He was a mountain climber, young and fit. He said if I gave him the job, he would guarantee to learn Portuguese in order to communicate with the Brazilian crew. He was cultured and intelligent, and I thought what a fine companion he would make out there in the wilds. I took a chance.

The film was hazardous and exhausting. We were cut off from help and back-up, but Philippe came through. Many fell, but he stood his ground. He made the forest look magical. I then took him to London to light the Blitz in *Hope and Glory*, for which he was nominated for an Oscar, and some years later we did *The Tailor of Panama* together. Three tough pictures, with our friendship and respect stronger than ever.

Leo the Last and *Where the Heart Is* were highly stylised movies, and I chose Peter Suschitzky to light them. He is subtle, sensitive and highly literate. His father is the distinguished photographer Wolfgang Suschitzky, and he could relate to the painterly references and political elements in these pictures. My Irish movies have been lit and operated by the urbane Seamus Deasy, who brings an air of charm and calm onto the set, which compensates for my tense and demanding manner.

Philippe, Peter and Seamus continue to survive and thrive, whereas my comrades – Phil Lathrop, Conrad Hall, Vilmos Zsigmond, Geoffrey Unsworth and Alex Thomson – are all dead. I salute them; they were at the heart of things, spinning stories out of light.

Movies are only a little more than a hundred years old, yet several generations of cameramen have come and gone. Digital shooting has made shots of any length possible, and we are now agog with admiration at the long Steadicam tracking shots of Emmanuel Lubezki in *The Revenant*, and at its astonishing director, Alejandro González Iñárritu, who is extending the scope of movie possibilities.

While I was preparing to make my last film, *Queen and Country*, Bob Chartoff called me and asked how it was going. I told him that some of the money had fallen out on that very day and the film was in danger of collapsing. He asked me how much. I told him, and that sum was in my account the next day. I dedicated the film to him: on the credits it says, 'For Robert Chartoff, with love and thanks.'

I had planned to make a trilogy of Shepperton movies. The first was to be about my mother and her three sisters, who were evacuated to Pharaoh's Island during the First World War, and their wild days as flappers in the 1920s; the second was *Hope and Glory*, in which my mother escaped with her children to the same stretch of the Thames during the Blitz; and the third concerned the two years of military conscription that tore me away from the idyll of the Thames. This became *Queen and Country*.

I had hit eighty. I had three scripts I still wanted to make, but time was running out. I had tried three times to make *Broken Dream*, about the end of the world and how the characters find a way of escaping into a parallel universe. It was an art film yet needed a commercial-movie budget, and so it always foundered for lack of money. *Halfway House* was a love story about a man grieving for the loss of his great love, whom he follows to a sort of clearing house where people first go when they die to edit the footage of their life. It was a reworking of the Orpheus legend. *Hostage to Fortune*, a thriller about a father and daughter, was set in South America and would have been too strenuous for my depleted physical powers.

So I opted for *Queen and Country*, another exercise in autobiography. It is set in the 1950s, a bleak decade in the aftermath of war. Food was still rationed, and Britain was broke. Yet youth is always optimistic. We hoped for an England where the class system had been swept away, along with royalty and privilege. After Churchill's heroics during the war, the British elected a Labour government led by the modest, self-effacing Clement Attlee. 'Attlee's taxi arrived and no one got out,' lampooned Churchill. Yet that short-lived Labour government founded the National Health Service and the secondary modern schools, where, for the first time, every child was taught something of music and art. Those kids grew up to be the Beatles and the Rolling Stones and David Bowie, part of the cultural explosion of the 1960s. None of those heroes came out of Eton. Before that time you either went to a grammar school and studied Latin and Greek, or you learnt a craft. What a pity Attlee's reforming government was not bolder. Had they swept away Eton, Harrow and all the other private schools that entrenched the ruling class, what a great difference it would have made. Even recently, David Cameron's cabinet was dominated by Etonians. Germany and France have high-quality state schools. There, if you say that your child goes to a private school, they ask what is wrong with him or her. If there are no private schools, the elite makes sure that the state schools are of high quality.

Queen and Country shows the older generation of soldiers clinging to Empire and imperial Britain, whereas we young conscripts could see that it was all going to change. Within a handful of years, the biggest empire the world has ever known was gone. Conscription and this period had never been put on film, so I set out to do so.

The conscripts are determined to skive and get through their two years of service, doing as little as possible, but they are under the authority of an NCO, Bradley, who insists on applying the letter of every army law. It emerges that the army functions only by getting around its own rules, or else ignoring them entirely. Bradley makes the lives of the conscripts unbearable, and they plot to overthrow him.

The limited money we were able to raise to make the picture meant that we had to build our sets in Romania, where we shot the entire film, except for three days on my beloved Thames at Shepperton. It had the shortest schedule and lowest budget of all my feature movies.

Queen and Country closely follows my time as an army conscript in the 1950s. I needed to cast actors to play my mother, father, older sister Wendy and myself, as well as the army characters. Casting is always difficult because you rarely find the actor who perfectly matches your idea of the character in the script. Each time you cast an actor, you give some part of the film away.

I saw many talented young boys, many of them just out of drama school. I found them alarmingly confident and collected. There was nothing of the awkward uncertainty that I remembered. We had all been through the war, the bombing and the privation. We were survivors, but vulnerable. I finally chose Callum Turner, who had no drama training. He had the task of playing a version of me, the long-dead youth that I was. He had been brought up by his mother and aunt, having never known his father. He was an acute observer, with a wry sense of humour. Casting the girls was easier. There were so many talented young actresses, but one, Vanessa Kirby, struck me with the force of recognition. She was my sister Wendy, wild, fearless, impulsive and, as I went on to discover, immensely talented.

Faced with the problem of reproducing the period, my first move was to lure production designer Tony Pratt out of retirement. He had done National Service and knew the times. We had worked together on many movies. Our first collaboration was on *Hell in the Pacific* in 1968. Tony was a storyboard artist, and since *Hell in the Pacific* had no dialogue, I hired him to storyboard the entire picture. It took us many weeks working together. I was impressed by his cine literacy, and even more by the fact that his uncle was Boris Karloff. I promoted him to production designer, his first job in a long and distinguished career. He worked in harness with a Japanese art director. Tony's father had died as a Japanese prisoner of war after the fall of Singapore, so working with a Japanese film crew was conflicting, as it was for Lee Marvin, who had fought them across the Pacific islands.

I chose Palau as the island where we would shoot the picture. It was very remote. I took Tony and Conrad Hall, the cameraman, out there to take a look. We boarded an old Dakota in Guam that battled its way through a hurricane to get us to Palau five hours later. The plane had taken a beating, but managed to land on the dirt strip. Conrad said, 'So far I love it.'

The next day we stood by a jetty, watching the girls in their floral Sunday frocks jump into the pellucid waters of the coral reef. They held their skirts out wide to trap the air and floated like blossoms.

Having been born in Tahiti, Conrad knew the light of the South Seas and how to avoid the overhead midday sun that flattened out the landscapes and rendered them bland. He taught me how to paint a scene with light. When I set up a shot, choosing the lens and the position of the camera, he would move it six inches to the left or right when my back was turned to make it his own, and I indulged him. He was a great companion and he loved making movies. He was the man you wanted by your side in the trenches, and he understood that – as Sam Fuller put it – film is war. I still have the scars from that picture, and some of them have never healed.

Tony was rather inhibited and shy around women at that time. As we stood watching the blossom girls floating on the water, with the bright coral beneath them, a girl surfaced bearing a harpoon, holding a fish in her mouth. With sleek and sensuous strokes she swam to our feet. Her saucer eyes regarded each of us carefully in turn, the fish twitching in its death throes. Finally making her choice, she dropped the fish in front of Tony. Conrad and I giggled, and Tony blushed. 'Thank you very much,' he said, in his very English voice. 'Awfully kind.' She led him away by the hand. He rejoined us the following morning, a changed man. It was his Gauguin moment.

Palau was a matriarchal society; only women could own land. The children took their mothers' names. The men had their canoes and fishing nets. They played, while the women got on with the serious business of life. I witnessed other young Palauan women choosing sexual partners with the same solemn intent as Tony experienced, and without the giggling and flirting we are accustomed to.

When the Americans occupied Palau after the Second World War, they tried to buy fish, but the men had no concept of fishing for more than the daily needs of their families. They had no use for the money that was offered. The Americans solved this problem by giving out free cigarettes. Once the islanders were hooked, they needed money to buy more, so they sold their fish. Capitalism had arrived in paradise.

The last shot of *Queen and Country* is of a 16mm wind-up film camera. It comes to a stop, my signal that it was my final film. I was eighty-one. It was at that point that I stepped aside, looked back and wondered if there was any meaning or pattern in my life, or was it – as it seemed – governed by chance?

THE GLEBE

It was 1969. I was doing post-production for my film *Leo the Last* in Ardmore Studios in Ireland. It was a fine summer, and my wife, Christel, and I fell in love with the nearby Wicklow mountains. We began to nurse the romantic notion of buying a holiday cottage and started to look around in a desultory way. An estate agent showed us a few places. One of them, the Glebe, was not a cottage, but a large eighteenth-century rectory in the village of Annamoe. A little river ran through the grounds. It was seductive but it was being auctioned the following day, so there was no time to get a survey to discover the almost inevitable wet and dry rot, and in any case it was much too big. I put it out of my mind.

We had been living in LA while making *Point Blank* and *Hell in the Pacific*, and although I had found the US liberating after the class-ridden negativity of England, it was beginning to drain my spirit. I didn't want to go on living there, nor did I want to go back to England.

The next day I found myself passing James Adams, the auctioneers, and there was the photo of the house in Annamoe in the window. Out of curiosity I went inside, to discover that the auction had already begun. I had a strange out-of-body experience. I was hovering in the ornate plaster ceiling, looking down on the events below. There were two people bidding for the house, and one of them appeared to be me. Suddenly, I was down among the mortals and being congratulated. Looking back, I marvel at the courage of Christel, who never bridled at my recklessness in abandoning the safety of the BBC to go off and try to make movies, or at my sinking every penny we had into that house.

We made firm friends in Annamoe. We would go into Dublin to see plays at the Abbey, the Gate and the experimental Project theatre (from which, years later, I cast many of the young actors for *Excalibur*), and every year we took the children to the Maureen Potter pantomime at the Gaiety Theatre.

Dublin was a friendly, easy-going city in the early 1970s. There were no underground car parks and one-way systems, and you could park your car on the street, which I did on one trip to the pantomime, leaving it as close to the Gaiety as possible. A scruffy urchin of about twelve confronted me. He looked me in the eye.

'Give me a quid and I won't scratch your car.'

I handed over a punt. It was before Ireland opted to join the euro.

'Give me another quid and I'll stop anyone else scratching it.'

Beguiled by his cheek, I paid up. He watched our four children tumbling out of the car.

'Where you going?'

I told him we were going to the pantomime.

'What's that?'

As it happened I had a spare ticket. One of my daughter's friends had bailed out at the last moment.

'Do you want to come with us?'

'I don't mind,' he said, with a shrug.

I asked him if it would be OK with his mother.

'I'm lucky. I don't have one, so I do what I like.'

Inside the theatre he stared at Maureen and her cast on the stage, and then looked at me as though I had tricked him.

'Them's real people.' It wasn't a proper movie.

You could send your children's names backstage, and Maureen would study them during the interval. In an astonishing feat of memory, she would come out and reel off the names of perhaps fifty or sixty kids. I had sent round the names of my kids and that of the boy's. When he heard his name called, he became shifty.

'How does she know I'm here?'

After the show, we went backstage to see Maureen. I told her the boy was supposed to be guarding my car. She loved his blatant self-interest.

The next day he turned up at the stage door and said he was a friend of Maureen Potter and he wanted a job. They gave him some chores and he hung around the theatre, becoming a fixture.

He grew up to be the stage manager.

SOLITUDE

Forty-five years later, I live alone in that very house so rashly acquired. It sighs and groans in the night. Its walls are arthritic; its floors drone a dirge to the trees that died for them. It wears the patinas of two wives and echoes with the voices of the seven children raised in it. The three young ones, the second litter, live with my former wife, Isabella. They come up at weekends, and the older ones when they can, but I jealously guard my newfound solitude.

I am a man I never had time to get to know. No introspection at the coalface. I suspected he was a fraud, a liar, full of hollow passion, best kept locked away. My belief was that identity is defined only in action, in what we do. I would always noisily claim that we exist only as metaphor. We have no more centre than a song, a painting or a poem. We occupy bodies we only partially comprehend. Occupy? What is this 'I' that is piloting this complex machine? A hollow, a vacuum, an absence, I would have said. I was on automatic pilot.

But lately I have spent much time with him. I can't say I like him, but since it is just the two of us, we are learning to get along. I have even found it possible to forgive him. He no longer embarrasses me, nor do I feel the need to apologise for him.

We are gradually merging together, the two of us, but paradoxically becoming less substantial, in danger of disappearing into a tree or a rock as we wander about this valley in the Wicklow mountains. The little river that runs through my land has bathed and baptised me for half a century, washing away my sins. Now, as I sit on its banks, it calls out, 'Come with me, come to the sea.' Tempting, but there is yet more to contemplate in the solitude. It draws me back to that shy boy, the father to the man.

BLOCKBUSTER

The bomb was a blockbuster. It pierced the roof of our next-door neighbour's house and made a gaping hole at the foot of Mrs Murgatroyd's bed, then buried itself deep under her living-room floor. Had it exploded and lived up to its name, it would have obliterated the whole of our suburban London street.

I like to think that some Polish slave labourer in a German munitions factory covertly sabotaged the detonator and allowed these words to be written. There was no air-raid warning. Did a German bomber pilot, straying from his squadron, in a fit of panic turn for home and dump his huge bomb not on the Houses of Parliament, but on our inoffensive 1930s semi-detached houses?

It was a few days before Christmas. I was eight years old; my sister, Angela, six. We were kneeling on the floor, gluing paper chains, which covered the carpet. When the bomb fell, the house shuddered and the blast wave bounced the paper chains up from the floor and they danced in the air, to our childish delight. Then with a shimmy and a sigh they fell back to rest.

Our father was home on Christmas leave from his mundane duties in the Royal Army Service Corps. That random clerk's tick beside his name had sent him to India in the First World War, while his classmates had all perished as subalterns in the trenches. Having had such a good time the first time round, he couldn't wait to join up again twenty-five years later. However, he was considered too old for action and was, crushingly, assigned a typewriter as his weapon. 'I'm typing for England,' he said bitterly.

So on that night he had the recklessness of a hero denied heroics, and next door's bomb was his apotheosis. He dashed out of our house into the pitch-dark street, bearing only a flashlight that had an obligatory black hood over its beam, which prevented light from escaping upwards towards our airborne enemies.

He found the front door of our neighbour's house swinging on one hinge. The windows were shattered and the curtains had been blown out through the gaps and were waving in the wind like hands calling for help. Mrs Murgatroyd lived alone and was a semi-invalid. My father ventured in and called her name. Her fluty voice answered, 'Who's there?'

'It's George from next door.'

He climbed the staircase, which had twisted into a semi-spiral shape. The hole at the foot of the bed had taken out most of the floor, but George was able – with the help of his torch – to edge his way around it to get to the bed. He carried Mrs Murgatroyd over his shoulder, down the twisted stairs and out past the swinging door and the waving curtains. He sat her down in one of our armchairs. 'What lovely paper chains. You have been busy,' she warbled. My mother handed her a cup of tea. 'I don't want to be any trouble,' she said.

By this time, air-raid wardens had gathered. They came into the house with their muddy boots and trampled on our paper chains. Crouched among those muddy boots, my sister and I wept. For us it was one of the great tragedies of the war, comparable to the destruction of Dresden.

My first big box-office hit as a film director was *Deliverance*. I phoned John Calley, the head of production at Warner Brothers, to ask him how it was doing. 'It's a blockbuster,' he said, and a little shiver went down my spine.

In the morning George went back into the damaged house. The bathtub was hanging from an electrical cable over the twisted staircase. A touch brought it crashing down. 'Hanging by a thread,' said my father to the admiring neighbours. He and my mother wore sombre faces, but inside they seemed to be in a state of feverish excitement. There were ominous cracks in our walls. The house was as unstable as my parents' marriage.

SHEPPERTON

My mother hated our arid suburban street and derived a guilty satisfaction from the destruction rained down upon it. 'Come, friendly bombs, and fall on Slough,' prayed Betjeman. She yearned for the bohemian freedom of her youth. Her father, having made his fortune from a gin palace in the London docks, had built a romantic Kashmiri bungalow on Pharaoh's Island, in the Thames. My mother and her three sisters grew up there during the First World War, escaping the attentions of the Zeppelins and the poverty of the Isle of Dogs. They lived lives of wild abandon that only wars allow children.

My father returned to his unit, and my mother fled with her children to Shepperton and her beloved river. There was the Pharaoh's Island of her youth and, a little further downriver, the lock and two weirs. Below the lock, the Thames widened as the River Wey joined it.

With the men away at war and the women working, we kids ran free, swimming and boating and foraging for food, eating moorhen's eggs and frying the fish we caught on open fires. No air raids, only a stray bomb dropped in the river that brought many stunned fish to the surface, a scene that found its way into *Hope and Glory*. Schools were shut for long periods for the lack of teachers. I fell into perfect harmony with the river.

> The old ferryman had always been there
> All the boy's life, and would be for ever.
> The horny hands grew out of the oar's wood,
> The wind-eroded face veined as weathered oak.

The blades barely ruffled the windless water,
Yet sent a trail of eddies spiralling back to shore,
Releasing the heady ozone from the deep
That the boy breathed in, inhaling the river.
The oars squeaked and polished the rowlocks,
Dip, pull, lift, dip.

A necklace of drops drip from the tip of the oar,
Each perfect sphere lives a moment's life,
Floating on the river's skin before falling back.

The boy drowns in a water reverie,
Entranced by the plop of drops on water.

Dip, pull, lift, drip, dip . . .

Trickling down from Cirencester,
The Thames gathers up creeks and meadow streams.
At Oxford it graduates to river status,
By Shepperton the water is weary and sluggish.

The fantasy of Pharaoh's Island parts it,
Confounds it with Kashmiri bungalows called Sphinx
    and Philae.

Scarcely rejoined and hardly settled back when
The lock and two weirs confront it,
Rough it up from its lazy ways, boil it alive.

Below, the River Wey joins it and offers up its water.

Together they swell and broaden and bear slowly down
On a ferryboat with an old man and a dreaming boy.

The ferryman rows the heavy skiff without effort,
Or with what small effort is required,
For by and by the boat slides across the Thames
To Weybridge on the other side of the world.

The boy was sent away to grow up.
When he came back the old man and the skiff were gone.

A chain ferry was in its place.
A rectangle of welded steel.
Flat-bottomed, it could carry bikes and prams.
A rough lout spun the wheel,
The chain screamed across it,
Churning water, dragging mud,
Tearing the river in two.

At ten years old, my little world – our wooden bungalow and
garden, the lock, a stretch of river – was so perfect, so far away from
the war that I began to develop the suspicion that it was a kind
of elaborate set. Spending so much time alone with my younger
sister I turned in on myself. I imagined we were the victims of
an experiment. People in the far future wanted to discover how
children responded to life and war in the distant past. My parents
were actors, as was the postman, my visiting grandparents and
the lock-keeper. We children were being observed as we lived in
this primitive environment. I kept a sharp eye out in the hope of

catching them at it. If I could turn a corner quickly, I might find the edge of this reconstruction and be back in the science-fiction future where I really belonged. Why had that bomb not exploded, for instance? Why had Mrs Murgatroyd not been more alarmed? The careless cruelty of the muddy boots was a test. Perhaps people in the future no longer cried or felt grief and wished to study these phenomena.

I was able to live out this fantasy only by ignoring or disbelieving the evidence to hand. For instance, my father's story that he had served in India was very suspect. India itself sounded made up, despite the elephant's-foot umbrella stand he claimed to have brought back with him. Then, one day, my father had one of his recurring bouts of malaria, the first I had witnessed. The musky heat coming from his bed was surely the authentic smell of India, and it convinced me, at last, that he had indeed served there. Strange that the most ephemeral of the senses should prove so convincing.

THE WAR WAS OVER. It was 1947. I was fourteen. The river flooded. It was a bitterly cold winter, and food and clothes were still rationed.

Riding home from school, the fire engine passed me with bells clanging. I pedalled hard to follow it. My sense of excitement was dashed when I saw it was our wooden bungalow that was burning. They asked me if anyone was inside. My sister, Angela, usually got back from school before me. A fireman was preparing to go into the inferno when Angela appeared, having gone to play with a friend. I was worried about my dog, but he came running up to me. The heat was so intense that the fruit trees in the garden were shrivelling, including the one next door that bore exquisite apples.

My mother bottled fruit for the winter and would store the glass jars on the wardrobe in her bedroom. They started to explode and fly up through the burning roof – yellow peaches, red rhubarb, fragments of crystallised glass. It was beautiful.

The fire was quenched by the time my parents returned. I picked my way over wet charcoal. I found the tin box that contained my lead soldiers. They had melted into a single lump.

We had only what we stood up in. 'At least we have each other,' clichéd my mother, but our food and clothing ration books had been burnt and we had nowhere to sleep. I remember feeling a lightness. I suppose I was light-headed. My father asked me what I was smiling about. He seemed far away. Having nothing seemed wonderfully liberating. Since that day I have owned only things that I would not mind losing. Perhaps that is why I surrendered so much to my wives. When I signed the divorce agreements, I experienced that same lightness.

We found a bungalow we could rent up the towpath. Someone made a collection for us. One person gave us a saucepan, another a knife and fork, and so on. It took weeks to get emergency ration books. My father did not have a bank account. His cash had burnt too. The war was over, but we were plunged into the condition of the displaced millions across Europe, dependent on friends and the kindness of strangers.

My mother rallied. She was indefatigable. She had always sewed and had made all our clothes, knitted our socks and sweaters, darned and mended. She just kept on doing it. She grew vegetables and made jam. We had no refrigerator, of course, but she preserved food for the winter. She cooked, made bread and had a part-time job. She did it all with grace, and Grace was the name I gave her in *Hope and Glory*. She always reminded me how fortunate we were

– she had lived through two world wars.

Like most women, my mother went to work for the war effort. My father's best friend, Herbert, employed her in his factory canteen. After the workers had been fed their lunch and the dishes were done, he would drive my mother back to Shepperton in his Armstrong Siddeley Sapphire, supplementing his meagre petrol ration with a sup of black-market stuff. They would sit in the car talking behind steamed-up windows. I kept a close watch on them as their love deepened.

My mother had a pale, tender beauty, and her melancholy pained me. When I was about six years old, I woke one night to the sound of what I thought were my mother's anguished cries. I opened her bedroom door a crack to see my father pounding away on top of her. I shut the door and wept bitter tears. Shortly after that, I found a cloth by her bed soaked in menstrual blood. She very gently explained the process, claiming that all women bled. Did she really expect me to believe such a preposterous story? It was obviously made up to protect my father's brutality. I became fiercely protective of her, and consequently, in later life, hopelessly susceptible to women wronged by callous lovers.

Herbert was a reassuring presence, wise and solid, whereas my father was erratic and exciting. Herbert had a way of clarifying the confusions of a young boy. I became very attached to him but jealous of my mother's affection for him and wary of his intentions.

As their relationship deepened, I became vaguely aware that I was somehow betraying my father. Once, when he was on leave, he asked me if Herbert was often at our house. I said he sometimes gave Mother a lift home, and I felt my face redden and saw the pain in my father's eyes.

In *Queen and Country* there is a scene where my eighteen-year-old surrogate, on leave from the army, sees his mother waving across the river at her one-time lover.

'Do you still see him?' the boy asks.

'No, we just wave.'

'I was ten. Do I betray my father or my mother?' says the boy to his mother.

That dilemma haunted me and has made me secretive. That I preferred Herbert to my father exacerbated my guilt.

Much later, I discovered the backstory. Herbert and my father, survivors of the First World War, were best friends and had served in India together. They were inseparable. My mother's father, Henry Chapman, had moved up from his gin palace in the London docks and now had a pub, the Alexander, at the foot of Wimbledon Hill. It was always packed with young men drawn to it by the four beautiful barmaids – my mother Ivy and her three sisters. Grandfather put up scrolled mirrors behind the bar so that his four daughters could be seen in multiple images of erotic abundance.

My father and Herbert were besotted with Ivy, and she was drawn to them. The two men were never apart, so she could hardly distinguish one from the other. They rode their belt-driven motor-bikes down to Shepperton, where they swam and boated with the girls. Little by little, Mother was drawn towards Herbert and away from George.

A million young men dead in the fields of Flanders had left a generation of spinsters and widows, but Ivy and her sisters were a fresh generation, the Charleston-dancing flappers of the 1920s. At the end of the war, besides the million dead, there were a further million under arms, and they were dumped onto a depressed labour market. George got a job, Herbert did not. He had nothing to offer Ivy, so he quietly withdrew. Ivy waited in vain, but it was only George who turned up at the pub, and she married him. Herbert was the best man.

Late in life, Herbert was besieged by arthritis and dependent on codeine. My mother was constantly at his bedside. With death's door ajar, she nursed him, her face luminous with love, all concealment abandoned, there for all to see as she eased his torrid pain with the opiate of love.

In all the years that followed, my father waited for that look to fall on him, but it never did. She loved him, but not enough – which is worse than not at all.

Even in her nineties she never forgot my birthday, but she often thought that she had. A card would arrive, and on the following day another would come. One year I got five. I often dream of her, and in those dreams she directs that look of luminous love at me.

Although embittered by never receiving that look from my mother, my father was by nature playful and easy-going, but when we children took advantage and overstepped the boundaries, he would fly into a rage and scare the hell out of us, as he did over the affair of the apple.

During the war there was no imported fruit, nothing out of season. I was twelve before I saw a banana. In the next-door garden was a tree that bore the sweetest, most addictive apples I have ever tasted. I would sneak in and scrump an apple every day. Then twice a day. Soon I needed three a day. The neighbours were mostly away, so there was nothing to impede my habit. My father caught me trespassing several times and demanded that I desist. The neighbours would soon return and see how depleted their tree was. But I could not stop.

'If you pick one more apple from that tree, I will thrash you,' he said.

The fear of the lash deterred me, but the craving became unendurable. I climbed the tree and ate the apples without picking them, leaving the cores hanging from the branches. My father was horrified. He failed to see the distinction between picking and eating.

In the final scene of my film *Excalibur*, I follow the legend and have the dead King Arthur transported by ship to Avalon, the Land of the Apple, from where it was promised he would return, renewed. Did he come back as an Apple Mac computer or an iPhone and conquer the world?

Last year, the apple trees in my orchard here in Ireland were so laden that some branches needed crutches to support them. This year the fruit is not so plentiful, although the orchard was drenched in blossom, like a fall of snow. Was it a late frost or an absence of bees? My neighbour, Danny Rochford, kept hives but gave up after his wife died – gave up everything pretty much. We read that all across the world bees are leaving their hives and not returning, giving up like Danny. Danny never wore a hood or gloves when he plundered the hives. His arms were covered in bees, but they never stung him. How were the bees able to differentiate him as benign and all other humans as a threat?

There is a tiny mite that loves to get into hives for the honey but is always repelled by the guard bees. The mites respond by clubbing together in their hundreds and forming themselves into the shape of a bee, thus fooling the guards. This requires a sophisticated organising intelligence, yet how can this be?

Although trees are made almost entirely of air and water, they do require some trace elements, particularly nitrogen. There are certain bacteria that are nitrogen fixers; that is to say, they can take nitrogen from the air and convert it into a form that living organisms can use. When these bacteria attach themselves to a tree, the tree will respond by producing carbohydrates to feed the bacteria, thus encouraging them to go on producing the nitrogen it needs.

These examples suggest an alternative intelligence that recognises, calculates and responds. We are told that a tree's life cycle – when to shed its leaves, when to bud – is regulated by a few hormones. In my new solitude I walk among the trees and try to divine their silent thoughts. As I write this, they are shedding their leaves, which dance joyously in the wind. Before letting them go, the trees withdraw their nitrogen, rendering them useless as manure.

My film *Hope and Glory* was the story of the Blitz, but also a hymn to the subtle glories of Shepperton, and in one scene it shows the boy, my surrogate, carefully lowering himself into the river one early morning, trying not to disturb the stillness of the surface. This derived from an experience I had at sixteen, two years after the fire. Exhausted by exams, I went upriver in my kayak, determined not to speak, not to use language, to give up words. After two silent days, the visual world began to take on a luminous clarity. The veins of a leaf, the seeds of a dandelion seemed miraculous. I camped on Runnymede, where the Magna Carta had been signed, a place of great resonance. I woke to a perfect stillness and knew that if I could enter the river without disturbing its glassy skin, why then I would live my life in a state of grace.

The reality was that I had just left school, and when I got back I was expected to get a job and earn a living. My secret dreams of being a writer and making movies seemed very remote. Yet my mother's gift of the portable typewriter gave substance to those dreams.

DROWNING

I was twelve when I fell into the Thames above the lock at Shepperton, the result, perhaps, of a moment's dizziness from a surfeit of apples. The four sluice gates were open, and I was sucked down. I struggled for the surface, but the down-pull was too strong. Onlookers begged the lock-keeper to close the sluices, but he refused on the grounds that if I were sucked down towards one of the sluices, the closing gate might impale me.

When I could no longer hold my breath, I let it go and inhaled the river. The lungs close off and the water is sucked into the stomach. I breathed the river, in and out, the water roaring in my ears. I stopped struggling. I opened my eyes. I let go. I understood I was drowning, and it was not unpleasant. I was simply becoming part of the river. I had become the river. This is where I belonged.

As the lock filled, the suction from the sluices ceased. The lock-keeper probed with his long pole and hooked me out. He pressed on my stomach and I spewed up the river. I never told my mother.

Whether or not it is connected to drowning, I have a need to be close to water. I ache for it, and my spirits fail if they are denied too long. At bad moments, in a despairing night, I can call up the Thames of my childhood and let it flow consolingly through a troubled mind. I feel compelled to immerse myself in any body of water I encounter and often have the urge to keep swimming out to sea and not turn back. The little river, the Avonmore, which flows through my land in Ireland is what seduced me into living here. I can see it from my bedroom window and hear it in the silence of the night. It is mostly shallow, but there is a swimming hole deep enough to dive into. I go there each summer's evening and bathe naked and alone. It is shrouded by ash, alder, birch and sally. Reflected in the river is an underwater wood of liquid trees.

Intent, posing as a stick,
The heron watches for fish.
A naked man stands on the bank,
Waiting to be invited in.
On days when he is unworthy,
The river will not have him.

Leaving himself behind,
He dives into the black water.
Embraced, forgiven, renewed,
He dries in the weak sun's light.
Does the fish feel the heron's bite?

How much pain can water take?
An ocean, a river, a lake?

ANNAMOE

My house is in the village of Annamoe, which can be found between prosaic Roundwood, which claims to be the highest village in Ireland, and the monastic settlement of Glendalough.

In Annamoe we have no church and no pub. For a while we had a shop that housed a post office, but that is now gone. The village was the home of the Barton family. Robert Barton was a signatory to the fateful treaty of 1921 that divided Ireland and provoked the civil war. His cousin, Erskine Childers, spent his childhood holidays in Annamoe and developed a deep affection for Ireland. He was a British army officer and a member of the court of St James. He was also the author of *The Riddle of the Sands*, which warned of Germany rearming before the First World War. So deeply did he sympathise with the Irish struggle for independence that he filled his yacht with arms, sailed to Ireland and joined the cause. This caused a great scandal in England, but the Irish rebels never quite trusted him and finally they executed him as a spy.

His young son, also named Erskine, visited him in jail on the eve of his execution. 'If people ask you how your father died,' he said, 'tell them that he died for Ireland.'

Young Erskine pledged to devote himself to the country and rose to the rank of Tánaiste, or deputy prime minister. One summer night while staying with the Bartons, he was taking supper at my house. He declined my offer of more wine, saying, 'I had better not have another because Jack Lynch [the prime minister] is away and I am in charge of the country.' He had an innocent pomposity that was widely ridiculed but which I found touching.

He eventually became president of Ireland and died in office from a heart attack while addressing the College of Surgeons. Is there a doctor in the house? Yes, about two hundred. Robert Barton was by then well into his nineties and not robust enough to attend the funeral in Dublin. I was deputised to take him up to the burial ground at Derrylossary, a stone's throw from Annamoe. There I noted with pleasure a recent grave where the dead one was described as 'Friend, Musician, Lover'.

Together, Robert and I looked down as the cortège approached, with military band playing and people lining the road. I remarked to Robert on the extraordinary outpouring of affection for Erskine.

'All the more extraordinary since there was no evidence of it while he was alive,' said Robert, in his dry manner.

It was Robert's horror of the damage alcohol had inflicted on Ireland that set him firmly against Annamoe having a pub, and he would not allow it. This was partially offset by nearby Roundwood having five pubs, all of which are still thriving.

It was the tradition of the Barton family that the elder son managed the estate in Annamoe, while the younger son went to Bordeaux and handled the wine business. They would buy up barrels of cheap new wine and ship them to Ireland. This eventually evolved into the Château Léoville Barton, one of the great *premiers crus*. I was at the vineyard once. Anthony Barton, who currently runs it, is very cynical about the pretentious nature of wine connoisseurs. 'What is wine after all?' he said. 'Just a brief interlude between grape juice and vinegar.'

Robert's cellar in Annamoe was well stocked with the family wine, and whenever I was invited for lunch the wine was of the highest order. Sadly, they had a butler who drank the cellar dry. Robert and his devoted wife would sit side by side at the end of the long dining table. 'We began to have our suspicions about him', Robert confided to me, 'when instead of setting the plates down before my wife and myself, he would shy them down the length of the table.'

Mary, Mistress of Post

Having no pub, no church, no post office, we were obliged to go to the next village to collect our mail and buy our ice cream and cigarettes. Mary arrived from the west, a dazzling dark-haired colleen with dancing blue eyes, the bride of a handsome Wicklow farmer.

She lived and served in the little village shop that was also the post office. She knocked us all sideways. Shy fellows were fearful of buying a stamp. At any moment, they felt, she might drag them across the counter and ravish them. She flirted and teased and wanted to know everything about everybody. Her appetite for gossip was insatiable, and when the dour villagers got wary of her and began to hold back, there were always postcards to read to find out where people were off on their vacations. We started to write little postscripts: 'Hope you enjoyed reading this, Mary' and 'Please deliver this, Mary, when you've finished with it.'

When a parcel arrived, her curiosity would get the better of her and she wouldn't be able to resist opening it. She would examine the contents, then seal it up and send it on. One day she opened a package and a lovely floral frock tumbled out. Surely there was no harm in trying it on. It was a perfect fit, and the low neckline gave her fine breasts the framing they deserved. She could not bear to take it off, so she kept it on. The addressee had plenty of dresses and wouldn't miss this one. Lost in the post. Unluckily, your woman had sent it back to change the size, so she knew the dress and was understandably miffed to find Mary wearing it in the shop and demanded it back. Mary found this attitude unreasonable, since it suited her so much better than the woman for whom it was intended. There were tears and other women came into the shop and all agreed how well Mary looked in the dress, and she in tears, and couldn't your woman see that, and didn't we all love Mary. The woman was abashed, and somehow Mary kept the frock.

After that it became a little easier to take an item from each parcel as a kind of tithe. She began to resent the effort involved in repacking each one. She would prevaricate, and the opened parcels would lie around. Some of them were gifts to children, and her own young daughters would fall upon the toys and she would forget which parcel they had come out of, and her girls would scream when she tried to recover the toys, but somehow it didn't seem to matter in the bigger picture. To dull her ardour, Mary had taken to the bottle, and sometimes when she was trying to repack a parcel it got into a tangle and she gave up on it.

When flowers arrived for someone, she just put them in a vase and stuck them in the shop window so that everyone could enjoy them, and not just that stuck-up woman for whom they were intended.

As her alcohol consumption increased, she started dipping into the till and was soon drinking the post office dry. It all blew up in her pretty face. Garda McGill was obliged to act, even though he had a very soft spot for Mary. The priest roared. The post office was closed, and Mary went to rehab. Chastened, she took to helping others to expiate her sins.

We all get our letters and parcels now, but how we miss her flighty ways and dancing smile.

The Synges

My house was formerly the Protestant rectory, and although Annamoe had no church, it was midway between the one in Derrylossary, where Erskine Childers is buried, and St John's Chapel of Ease in Laragh, and the rector had to straddle the two.

Dr Sam Synge, brother of the poet J. M. Synge, was rector here in the 1930s. He had been a medical missionary in China for some years and took up this living when he returned. He practised Chinese medicine in Annamoe, and I suspect that he was more converted to Chinese beliefs than the Chinese were to his Christianity, since he was famous in Annamoe for his sermons that never exceeded five minutes. I learnt this history from his eccentric son, John, who was brought up in my house. John was a great linguist and had mastered African as well as European languages. He believed there was a common root to all languages and was on a quest to find it. He could read an Indian or Persian carpet like a book. He was very intense and had no small talk. One evening he arrived at my house for supper. He was very excited and announced to the other guests that he had passed through zero on that very day. To the startled guests he explained that the concept of zero was an abstraction, an absence, nothingness. By passing through it he was able to experience the nothingness that existed or failed to exist before the universe was created. It silenced our trivial gossip.

Laragh

Where the holy Glendalough River collides with our pagan Avonmore River stands the scrawny village of Laragh. Laragh is a place from which you can get to other places. Follow the confluence of those rivers and the road twists and dips and skips through glorious oak woods, past the pretty Clara Lara to righteous Rathdrum.

The coaches full of pilgrims pass through Laragh on their way to Glendalough, the holiest place in Ireland and not ten Hail Marys away from Laragh. Or, if you veer right before you reach Glendalough, the road will take you on a switchback ride over the mountains to the Wicklow Gap and then down to the Dublin road on the other side.

Laragh is on the way to somewhere else, an inhabited signpost, but it has its secrets. Hidden in a dank wood is St John's, a chapel of ease, not quite a church for somewhere that is not quite a place. St John's is so small that when my daughter Katrine was married there, her train was longer than the aisle, so that her bridesmaids were, for a spell, left outside.

Nearby, in an even danker wood, is Laragh Castle. If St John's is modest, then the castle is apologetic: the smallest castle in all of Ireland, a castellated doll's house. This was the domain of the Stuart family. Francis Stuart was a promising young writer and a protégé of Yeats, who, as we know, famously fell in love with Maud Gonne. She provided the unrequited love so vital to a poet. Maud had a beautiful daughter, Iseult, and Yeats fell in love with her too, but she also rejected him.

Iseult led an adventurous life that included an affair with Ezra Pound. When she married Francis Stuart – seven years her junior – Yeats took it badly and revised his view of the young writer. He wrote:

> A girl who knew all Dante once,
> Lived to bear children to a dunce.

She bore Francis three children: two girls and a boy, Ian. They lived in Laragh Castle, in near penury. It was the 1930s, and war was brewing. To earn a little money, Francis did a lecture tour in Germany and was offered the job of lecturer in English literature at Berlin University. He went back there in 1940, after the Jews had been rounded up. Controversially, he broadcast Nazi propaganda to the people of neutral Ireland. Iseult struggled on with the children in the castle.

The Germans decided to drop a spy into Ireland. They sent him to Francis for a briefing. Francis apprised him of the habits and customs of his compatriots and suggested that when he got to Ireland, would he look up Iseult and tell her that her husband was well, since he couldn't contact her.

The spy was parachuted in and eventually made his way to Laragh and the castle. Iseult invited him into the house, and very soon into her bed. He stayed for some weeks, before the neighbours got suspicious and he was carried off and interned.

After the war, Francis came back to Ireland, to a mixed reception. Meanwhile, his son, Ian, after studying and living in London, had become a notable sculptor, and his homing instinct found him back in Laragh. He brought with him his pregnant lover, Anna.

Apart from the apologetic Church of Ireland chapel, Laragh has a big, brash Catholic church. Glendalough has seven medieval churches clustered about the ruins of the monastery, and not one of them is open for business. The few souls who live in Glendalough are obliged to attend Mass in Laragh.

A new priest arrived in Laragh, not the usual rough country priest but a sensitive, idealistic young fellow, Father Barry. Sensing weakness, the parishioners treated him with disdain. He and I became friends, and he often came for supper and we played chess.

That he would visit a house that was once a Church of Ireland rectory drew further strictures.

Anna duly gave birth to a daughter, Laragh, named for the village. This was a great scandal in those times since Anna and Ian were unmarried. Fr Barry saw it as his duty to visit Anna, despite the scandal it would cause. He was shy and nervous, but brave. Who shall cast the first stone, and so on.

Anna was breastfeeding when he arrived, and the celibate young priest was confronted by a glorious exposed breast. Anna was amused by his confusion.

'I have so much milk, Father,' she said coyly. 'Would you care for a cup?'

He arrived at my door ashen-faced and recounted the story. He was shy around women and his vow of celibacy sheltered him from them, but he had seen a vision of the glories he was forgoing.

Shortly after this, he departed for a mission in Africa. He had inherited some money. He gave it all to the needy of Laragh and left no address where he could be thanked.

Scots and Lee

When Father John Maguire, my teacher and mentor, came to stay, his presence in a former Protestant rectory caused suspicion. When he sought permission from the parish priest in Roundwood to say Mass in his church, he was asked to provide evidence of his priesthood.

One of his visits coincided with the making of *Zardoz*, and he delighted his fellow Scot, Sean Connery, with his stories of a childhood in the Gorbals, while Sean capped him with poverty in Edinburgh. Lee and Pamela Marvin turned up, and John

entertained them all prodigiously. He kept a joke book for inject-
ing humour into his sermons.

On another occasion when Lee was staying, we invited the
rather stiff and formal next-door couple to supper. They brought
his mother, a formidable dowager. The atmosphere at the dining
table was rather strained because Lee had been drinking all day,
and he was sat with his head slumped on the table. As always, his
wife, Pam, tried to compensate for Lee's absence by chattering to
our guests, but Lee's great white-haired head cast a pall over the
occasion, and the conversation kept drying up or petering out.
The dowager, affronted by Lee, began making oblique comments
about manners. She was rigid and uncompromising.

Lee's head rose from the table. He looked blearily at the dowager. She looked down her nose at him contemptuously. Lee got
her into focus.

'Has anyone ever kissed your cunt?' he asked.

She drew herself up, stared back with flared nostrils. Unexpect-
edly, she smiled.

'As a matter of fact, they have.'

'They?' said her startled son.

We all laughed at his discomfort, then he laughed at himself,
and the party came to life. Suddenly, it was possible to say anything at all, and we did. Lee got away with this kind of prank because there was no malice in the man, but also an acute sensitivity.
He hated pomposity. He saw it as his role in life to puncture it.

Our Druid

Every place in Ireland has its own brand of oddity, each one different, but some things they have in common. They all have the

man who sits alone at the end of the bar nursing his pint. He is the sentinel: he keeps watch; he takes his drinking seriously. It is his duty. Then there are the clichés: the harmless drunk, the busybody.

But not many places have a Druid. Ours is Marcus Losack. He was a Church of Ireland vicar, but his researches into the origins of Christianity in Ireland led him back to an earlier time. He will conduct a wedding under the greensward or douse your baby in the holy waters of Glendalough.

He recently published a book about St Patrick, whose saint's day is celebrated throughout the world, a tribute to Ireland's greatest export – people. Patrick is noted for bringing Christianity to Ireland and for casting out the snakes. The Druid's book clarifies what we have always known: that when Patrick arrived in Ireland, there was already a bishop in place who would have had many priests in his see. As for the snakes, there never were any. Brendan Behan said that the cast-out snakes swam the Atlantic and turned into New York Irish cops.

Little is known of Patrick. Was he a Roman, as his name would suggest? A spurious biography was written a hundred years after his death describing miracles he had performed. It was a PR job.

Paddy's Whistle

My neighbour to the west is a musician – the irrepressible Paddy Moloney, chief of the Chieftains. His wife, Rita, expresses her love for him with a continuous torrent of abuse. He drowns her out with jigs played on the tin whistle he is never without. He gave a whistle to a female American astronaut, who took it up with her and learnt to play it while circling the Earth at eight kilometres a second. She mastered it well enough to busk along with them on their fiftieth-anniversary tour.

Adolf's Ear

Adolf Bader came to Annamoe a year or two before me. He has a hill farm just above my place. At ninety-five he runs it single-handedly. His beef cattle fetch a premium at market because they are always so well finished. He lets them live as families in the woods. He was tagging a calf the other day when the mother cow trampled him to the ground and tore his ear off with her hoof. He picked it up, got in his car and drove to the hospital. He presented the ear and asked them to sew it back on. You can hardly see the stitches. For a man wounded in the Battle of Stalingrad, this was a minor matter.

In nearly half a century he has had five or six sheepdogs. Only the first one needed to be trained. As a dog got old and slowed up, Adolf would acquire a pup to run with the old dog, and it would learn from it. In this way the knowledge has been passed down.

Unless I was away making movies, and rain permitting, Adolf and I played tennis every weekend for forty-five years. In his farming journal he would put a plus or a minus, depending on if he won or lost, so there is a record of our games, together with calves born, sheep sheared and hay made.

Luggala

My little river runs down from Lough Tay, where Garech Browne had his house, the magical Luggala. Mountains rise up from the lake. His exquisite gothic house would invite you into another impossible dimension. To enter it was to abandon your world and enter his. There, despite his reduced circumstances, he maintained it as a haven for musicians and poets who often came to lunch and stayed for a month. Then there were the landed and stranded gentry, who could be found wandering the corridors. Garech could be spotted, elaborately dressed, with his wispy white beard, walking in his deer park or examining his exotic trees. The trees I plant are mostly indigenous, but if a species was impossible to come by, that's the one Garech had to have.

Fifty years ago, he rescued traditional Irish music from extinction. His Claddagh Records recorded all the great old pipers and singers and fiddlers, and in founding the Chieftains he helped to bring Irish music back into popularity. At a Luggala lunch, a piper would always be on hand.

He was a collector. His library was a repository of Irish books, mostly first editions, a record of a nation's imagination. He was pathologically late. In forty years, I never knew him to have arrived on time, and not once was it his fault.

'Don't you own a watch?' I asked him one time, irritably.

'Yes, I have a collection of watches.'

'Where are they?'

'I keep them in the safe.'

By locking Time away, he sought to free himself from its strictures.

He became a Hindu in order to marry Princess Purna of Morvi. He had a long fascination with India, particularly the Raj. He and his wife lived apart for many years but remained faithful friends. I said to him once, 'Garech, you didn't marry a woman, you married a subcontinent.'

His father, Lord Oranmore and Browne, patriarch of a Norman family from the west of Ireland, drank as heavily as Garech and lived to be a hundred. He was the longest-sitting member of the House of Lords, 'sitting' being the key word, since in those seventy-odd years no debate moved him to stand and speak. Garech's mother, Oona, was a Guinness heir.

Garech always said that he wished he had never been born, which is why he never wanted to have children. He would have been imposing the life sentence on them that he himself endured.

Philip Giles did some decorating for me and for Garech. He was up a ladder at Garech's house once, painting a wall, and was a little embarrassed when at eleven one morning Garech appeared in his dressing gown, holding a glass of vodka. To cover his discomfort, Philip said, 'Ah, there's nothing wrong with a drink. Even Our Lord had a drink at the Last Supper.'

'Wouldn't you need a drink,' said Garech, 'if you knew you were going to be crucified the next day?'

Garech was meticulous about how he dressed and went to great lengths to secure the perfect cloth, the perfect cut. He would travel to Burma to buy the exquisite silk that he needed for his shirts. He insisted that his tailor maintained the highest standards.

My son, Charley, at the age of fifteen, got drunk at Luggala and threw up on a precious carpet. Gerry Hanley, the novelist celebrated earlier in these pages, observing the event and referring to the fact that Guinness money had financed Luggala, said, 'Don't worry, Charley, this house was built on vomit.'

The following morning I made Charley ride his bike to Luggala to apologise.

'That's a hard ride with a hangover,' said Garech. 'You had better come inside and have a drink.'

Garech and I were devoted but ill-matched friends, he the aristocrat, I the commonest of commoners. While he was always late,

I am always on time and the first on the set. I am carelessly dressed; he was impeccable. I am a republican who comes from a kingdom; he was a royalist who came from a republic. I am a workaholic; he was an alcoholic. Wherever I was shooting in the world, Garech would turn up to offer support, but he was always disappointed that I could not stop shooting to have a leisurely lunch with him. I left school at sixteen; he left much earlier than that. When he was sent to boarding school, he lasted only a few days. He walked down to the local post office and sent the headmaster a telegram purporting to be from his mother demanding that he come home immediately. He never went back. But despite a non-existent education, he was widely and deeply read, and his views were always well informed. He carefully distinguished between the good and the excellent.

Luggala cast a spell over all who encountered it. Seamus Heaney said, 'I think it is a case of crossing the border once you enter that glen. Once you start going down, you do cross a line into a slight otherworld. And when the house appears there's a sense of destination.' It was often said that whatever happened at Luggala did not count in the outer world.

John Huston arrived at Luggala in the dead of night. He awoke to the view from his window of the lake and the folds of the hills that frame it. He was enchanted. I met him there and was captivated by his urbane manner and his devotion to living the good life. Wounded by Hollywood, he had long since decided that there were more important things in life than movies. Yet from time to time he would commit deeply to a project. One such was *Fat City*, about a small-time, washed-up, alcoholic boxer, played by Stacy Keach. By that time Huston had elected to live in Ireland and was riding to hounds with the Galway Blazers. He had just finished

Fat City and he invited me to watch a screening of it in Dublin. Muhammad Ali was fighting in the city that night, and Huston invited him too. Ali arrived with his mother, a beautiful woman, and an entourage. After about ten minutes, Ali called out, 'I'm fighting tonight and you show me this movie about a loser?' He then started to talk back at the screen, and kept up a continuous commentary in his famous quick-witted style until the end of the movie. Huston sank deeper and deeper in his chair as Ali lacerated the film.

The picture opened to good reviews but poor business. I met Huston a little later. He said, ruefully, 'I wish I had recorded Ali's commentary and put it on the picture. It would have done a lot better.'

Huston's final film was set in Ireland: his adaptation of James Joyce's *The Dead*. It was wonderful. As I contemplate doing another film at a great age, I am inspired by his courage in making that movie from a wheelchair, with an oxygen tube up his nose.

I once had lunch at Luggala with Robert Graves. After the meal, some of the other guests went to view a place of magic: a grotto. Graves declined to join them. 'That's not the business of a poet,' he said.

'What is the business of a poet?' I asked.

'Falling in love,' he said, without hesitation.

I thought of his war memoir, *Good-Bye to All That*. On reconnaissance in no-man's-land, he was crawling on his belly towards the German trenches, but when the machine guns started up, trained low on the top of the British trenches, he had to jump to his feet so he would risk being hit in the ankles, not the head.

The others returned from their magic place, and I started telling a story about Luggala. Graves interrupted. 'I'm going to bed.

Wake me up if something interesting occurs.' Somehow I stuttered to the end of my tale.

One of the pleasures of having Garech as a neighbour was that he allowed me to swim in his lake, Lough Tay, whenever I wished. Next to the lake stands the tomb of his brother, Tara, the golden boy of the 1960s, dead at twenty-one. It imposes an air of tragic melancholy that Garech never quite escaped.

How Paul Fell on His Feet

Garech's lake flows into Lough Dan, which in turn feeds the Avonmore River that passes through my place on its way to my land neighbours, Paul McGuinness and his wife, Kathy Gilfillan. Straight out of Trinity University, Paul worked on my film *Zardoz*. He was in charge of transport. I arrived at my chosen location in the Wicklow mountains to find the trucks parked where I intended to shoot. I vented my displeasure on Paul and demanded that he move them. He said, 'Wouldn't it be quicker to turn the camera away from the trucks?' As this was his first job, I should have patiently explained that I had chosen that aspect because of the direction of the light and the ominous folds of the mountains. I should have acknowledged his lateral thinking and his initiative. Instead, I advised him to find another career.

He took my advice and managed a young pop group. They were struggling and only the financial support from Kathy, who had a good job as a copywriter in an advertising agency, kept them going.

The band was U2, and they made Paul very rich indeed. He bought the grand Avonmore House, just downriver from me, where he generously entertains his guests with fine wine, good fellowship and fireworks. He is lavish and spontaneous, whereas Kathy is cautious and considered – a fine balance. She has transformed the estate into something beautiful and productive. Her garden vegetables support Paul's *premiers crus* at their frequent lunches.

DYING FRIENDS

Jeremy Williams

The year 2016 arrived, one I never imagined reaching, my eighty-third. Over the Christmas holiday, two friends died: the brave cameraman of *Deliverance*, Vilmos Zsigmond, and Jeremy Williams, the architect. Jeremy went out to get a newspaper on Christmas Eve, but got a heart attack instead.

Jeremy designed my conservatory and the little bridge we built across the river. He helped plan the groves of trees I planted. He was a prodigious talent, but scatter-brained and disorganised. He had an ingratiating manner and an apologetic charm. His narcolepsy always betrayed him at the dinner table, often when I was in the middle of a tale. He died without the comfort of a priest, but how he received the last rites is worth telling.

Late one night he dozed off in his car and collided with a lorry packed with live sheep. He was thrown out of the vehicle and landed on the road, covered in blood, out cold. It was a dark night on a lonely road. This being Ireland, the first person to arrive was not a doctor, but a priest. Jeremy, recovering from the shock, began to assess his injuries as the priest intoned the last rites. He found he could move his toes and fingers. He remembered reading somewhere that when you are fatally injured, you feel no pain. Hearing the drone of extreme unction, he assumed he was dying.

More help arrived. Jeremy had been delivering some eighteenth-century dresses to the Irish Georgian Society. Someone covered him with one of them. The priest continued to pray over his inert body, while sheep from the damaged truck wandered the night street. Despite the copious blood, Jeremy realised that he was not hurt at all: the blood was from the sheep he had killed. However, he was much too polite to interrupt the priest and waited for him to finish. He then sat up, thanked the priest profusely and commended him on his delivery of the ritual.

Paolo Tullio

Paolo of the massive mind is dead. He was my neighbour for thirty years, just across the river. His door was always open, and he welcomed visitors with great warmth as he put the coffee on. His friends felt free to drop by. It was never inconvenient for him; he always seemed to have time. He sometimes opened the door in his dressing gown at noon, but you were still welcome. The son of Italian immigrants, he was a brilliant student at Trinity. He drove a red sports car, in which he took Trinity girls to his family home and showed them a faked family crest bearing the legend '*Semper Erectus*'.

Paolo knew everything – history, philosophy, politics, culture. Paolopedia, we called it. Before Google, he was essential in our lives. This massive mind resided in a sceptical Italian body. He was of short stature, but his large belly and huge head gave an illusion of size. His full head of hair was heroically swept back, and a rich beard completed the impression of a very large man compressed into a small body.

He was much too Italian to hold strong views or believe in anything. He ran a restaurant in Annamoe, but we are far out in the Wicklow hills and the strict laws against drunk driving finally did for him. 'I am unemployable,' he said to me.

This was not necessarily a bad thing in Paolo's book. It meant it was futile for him to look for work at his age. He could devote himself to the unalloyed pleasures of living his life and entertaining his envious friends, who were driven by ambition or the need to feed families. His children were grown, while his wife's painting drew her ever further to the west of Ireland.

He sold the restaurant and applied for planning permission to build a house on his land. Sometime previously, he had acquired some large boulders and he decided to build a stone circle. I had helped him, and we had aligned the stones to the winter and summer solstices and the compass points. Paolo claimed it was the first stone circle built for six thousand years. When the planning officer came, he inspected the land and refused permission on the grounds that it was a megalithic site. Paolo had taken the precaution of placing a modern coin under each boulder, so he was able to tip one over to reveal a euro to the astonished officer.

He wrote a book about his family home in Italy, *South of Rome, North of Naples*, and made it into a TV documentary. He knew all about mushrooms and harvested their many varieties, including magic ones, from our woods and meadows. He wrote a novel, *The Mushroom Man*, which delved further into the fungal mysteries. He built a pizza oven and a smokehouse, but he did not count any of this as work nor did it earn him any money. How he got by was a mystery.

His highly developed taste buds got him an offer from a national newspaper to write a weekly restaurant review. Since this could be done in a single day, he took it on, and I kept him company on some of those jaunts. His reviews were kind, too kind. He knew how hard it was to run a restaurant.

A radio station invited him to do a weekly slot answering listeners' foodie questions. People were astonished at the inexhaustible fund of ad hoc knowledge that could be summoned up from his massive mind. He was drafted into a TV version of this show. His amiable manner and easy charm soon turned him into a national treasure. To his horror he soon found he was working up to three days a week, but like all lazy people he found quick and easy ways of doing this – all of it managed by a tiny portion of the massive mind. For mental press-ups, he raced through the cryptic cross-word before lunch each day. He had an unlimited supply of silly jokes, which he delivered in a range of accents – an ability that encouraged me to cast him in two of my films. Paolo, the actor, never asked me about his motivation; he was the least motivated man I ever met. The only thing he took pride in was that he had never been beaten at Trivial Pursuit.

If I raged about some contentious political or social issue, he would summarise it accurately and calmly, and without indigna-tion or enthusiasm. As Yeats put it, 'The best lack all conviction, while the worst are full of passionate intensity.'

We saw each other most days, and it was always a pleasure to be in his affable company, though we seldom had an intimate conver-sation. He was a comforting, undemanding friend, always ready to excuse my inadequate excesses. He was acutely aware of the pre-carious nature of life and the futility of struggling against the cruel imperatives of chance. We laughed a lot at the absurdities around us. We were in a small boat together and Annamoe was a sheltered harbour, but the turbulent seas would capsize us in the end, and we hoped to go down laughing.

After the many dinners we shared, he could often be persuaded to pick up his guitar and sing sentimental Italian songs, in a reson-ant voice that was both authentic and self-conscious parody. He was a comforting, reassuring friend, a warm fire of a friend, some-one to sit by and find solace in the dancing flames.

His kidneys eventually let him down and he endured years of dialysis. I visited him in hospital shortly before he died. He said, 'I can't hug you, but I hug you in my heart.'

It is hard to accept that the massive mind has been extinguished, all those philosophical concepts and silly japes gone for ever.

'A cosmic joke,' he would have said.

John Montague

My friends fall away, leaving me stranded. Just before Christmas 2016 the great Irish poet John Montague succumbed. I delivered the eulogy at his funeral. Five famous poets rose from their pews and attested to his greatness by quoting a line each from his work. I read his poem 'The Locket', which tells the story of his abandonment. Born in Brooklyn, his impoverished parents sent him back to Ireland at the age of four to be brought up by an aunt. He never heard from his mother again, except for a brief encounter when he sought her out at the age of fifteen. When she died, he discovered that the locket she always wore contained a picture of him as a baby.

I admired the great range of Montague's subject matter – love, grief, loss, celebration. 'The Rough Field', a long, epic poem, was an anthem for Northern Ireland, in all its tough and mean ways, yet it was written with reluctant love.

A few weeks after his death I attended the launch of his last posthumous book of poems. I was surprised to find it included a poem dedicated to me. It was about my swimming hole, where he had swum with me from time to time. It was written from the point of view of a kingfisher.

Kingdoms

Standing buck naked
in his own sun-warmed
stealth of river,
a blue arrow
swerves near:

a kingfisher!

The spirit of the river
come to inspect, to query
this other, this blue-eyed monster
who dares to occupy
the same realm of stream and sky.

JOHN MONTAGUE

NATURE

In old age so many of the things I took for granted in my youth I now ponder and wonder at. Walking was once automatic; now I have to give precise instructions to my legs for each step, otherwise they wobble or wander off course. I watch these strange mammals precariously balancing on their hind legs. They chatter into their telephones. In restaurants they shout and roar with laughter. 'When I hear laughter,' said Baudelaire, 'I hear the roar of the wild beast.' Now that my hearing is failing me, it becomes merely an alien cacophony.

Because I no longer have the distractions of solving invented problems, I am constantly aware of living in a complex, unfathomable planet that functions independently of – and with great indifference to – us. In the margins, we interfere but have little effect. We warn ourselves that we may destroy the planet. I used to grieve over the destruction of the Amazon rainforest. Much of it grows over sand, so it is impossible to replant, but I realised that it was our problem, not Nature's. Nature could reinstate the rainforest in about four thousand years – a quick fix by its standards. We have the ability to destroy ourselves, not the planet. It will shrug us off and reinvent itself in another form of beauty.

Nature seems to be governed by laws and complex mathematics, yet water, of which we are made, seems exempt from these laws. It is as if water has cast a spell on scientists so that they don't investigate it. It is exempt from the rules. Don't ask why. It's too embarrassing.

Have any societies worshipped water, I wonder? Holy lakes and rivers, yes, but water as an abstraction? People have worshipped the effects of water, but not water itself. During my Catholic schoolboy experience, I used to study the holy water in those little enamelled troughs that hung on the wall of the chapel. You dipped your finger in and crossed yourself. Here was a magical mystery: a priest could pray over ordinary water and invest it with spiritual power.

In my youth, I scarcely gave water a thought. It was everywhere. It came out of a tap. It was anonymous, transparent, tasteless, without colour or smell. It was so characterless, it hardly existed, a wet nothingness.

Now I find water utterly fascinating.

Water

How does sap go up a tree,
Defying gravity?
Why does water expand
When it turns to ice?
Blood, sap, water,
The liquids of life.

Water comes from outer space,
And keeps coming every day,
Meteors of ice,
Riding on cosmic dust.
Extraterrestrial,
It brought life,
But how much more,
In the mystery of flow,
Is in that H_2O?

My well sucks water from the deep.
How long has it lain there?

Did it seep down
From the melting glacier?

Rain gathers oxygen as it falls,
They cleave like lovers
In pairs of molecules.

Inert,
Transparent,
Tasteless,
It can carry
Minerals,
Vegetation,
Gases,
And by dilution
Render poisons
Harmless,
So long as it flows.

But stagnant,
Dammed,
Deprived of oxygen,
It cannot breathe.
Its passengers
Expire.

Ubiquitous,
Mysterious,
Giver of life,
Healer,

God sent?

I was taught at school that sap rose by capillary action. These tubes were so narrow that the surface tension of water was sufficient to drag all those gallons of sap up a tree. Even at fourteen I found that preposterous.

Joel Coen emailed me the other day to say he was up in northern California, among the giant redwoods. Knowing my interest in trees, he wondered if I knew how the sap got from their roots to the top of their three-hundred-foot height.

There have been several theories, none of them convincing. One suggested that molecules of carbon dioxide acted like corks and pushed the sap upwards. Nonsense. Another idea is that as moisture evaporates from the leaves, a tiny vacuum occurs, and when multiplied by a hundred thousand the vacuum is strong enough to pull up the sap. The problem is that sap rises most vigorously in the spring, before the leaves come out.

The life cycle of trees is controlled by hormones that no one knows much about. Sap is water in disguise, and it shares its mystery and behaves in ways that defy the laws of physics. I am on a quest to find the answer before I die.

As I approach the end of my life and observe my progressive decrepitude, I enjoy an ease, and occasionally enlightenment, which comes from no longer having to defend a belief to myself – the Christianity I was born to, the humanism I adopted, and my seduction to the animism of the tribe I lived with in the Amazon. The ease comes from not having to struggle with the awkward contradictions that belief systems throw up. When I am alone with silence, I become aware of the empty room that God used to occupy. If I listen carefully in that empty room, I can sometimes hear water dripping, then flowing, and occasionally the roar of the deluge. Why is our planet awash with water, while the other planets in our solar system have none or very little?

This anomaly is the strongest case for divine intervention. The disciples of chance will argue that if a monkey tapping on a typewriter for a few thousand years will eventually come up with the works of Shakespeare, what are a few billion gallons of water? My hunch is that many mysteries are hidden in water.

I sought to conquer. I spent my life swimming upstream; now I go with the flow. I needed to know everything; now I know little and understand less. Who was it who said, 'My dog doesn't understand the universe, why should I?'

I went to a Catholic school, where I was taught by priests, but on Sundays I sang with the choir in the Protestant church of St Nicholas, in Shepperton. They both claimed to be the true faith, but how could that be? They could not both be right. One of them must be wrong. The mystery of the Mass and the heady smell of incense would draw me towards Catholicism, then the shaft of sunlight through the stained glass of the west window and the psalms at Sunday evensong would capture me. I was deeply troubled by this dilemma.

One summer's day I was drifting in my boat on the Thames, pondering this mighty dilemma, when the sun burst through the tendrils of a weeping willow with the blinding light of revelation. There was another possibility: what if they were both wrong? A great weight lifted from me and I floated up over the water, at last at one with my true nature, Nature itself. I prostrate myself before it, in awe of its beauty, humbled by its mysteries, fearing its wrath.

Socrates argued that in the womb we know everything, and that learning is rediscovering the knowledge we forgot at birth. When I was young and in a state of grace, I sometimes knew – or imagined – that all wisdom was available to me. Like many writers,

I occasionally feel that I am taking dictation, and that my work transcends my limits, is beyond me. What is this 'beyond'?

I have always been drawn to trees, but the more I study them in my later years, the more miraculous they seem (vide the nitrogen fixers above). I now treat them with respect and awe – even love. Science can only separate carbon from carbon dioxide or hydrogen from water at the expense of huge amounts of energy, a process that every leaf accomplishes silently and effortlessly through photosynthesis, building its tree with hydrocarbons and releasing oxygen into the air.

The weather forecasters apologise when they predict rain, yet how long would we survive without it? I am asked why I left sunny California for rain-drenched Ireland. I never trusted the weather over there. Their rain falls on other people a thousand miles away, up in the Rockies. It roars down the Grand Canyon and then is piped to the swimming pools and golf courses of LA. This precarious arrangement is failing, and California is suffering drought.

I never cease to be amazed by the process of the evaporation of oceans, the formation of clouds and the convenient winds that carry them here to Ireland. In Ireland, showers of rain fall out of blue skies and make rainbows. Low clouds envelop us up here in the Wicklow mountains and we get soft, misty rain that caresses the skin. At the other extreme, severe thunderstorms bombard us with icy hailstones; sometimes in summer they settle like snow. The skies can darken and steady rain set in for days. The river swells, and we stay inside and light the fire. Out of clear skies a quick shower reminds us that rain is still serving us, making crops grow and keeping us alive.

I am hemmed in by trees, crowded by them, dwarfed by them. I have become aware of the continuous conversation that Nature conducts, in a foreign language that I am trying to understand.

The wind blows and rustles the leaves, and that stimulates growth. Photosynthesis accelerates and the air is flooded with oxygen, but not for long because the proportion of oxygen in the air remains constant – forest or city. No one knows why, but it allows animals to breathe. When the wind drops, trees rest, become heavy, and I experience their drowsiness. Roots seek out water and send it up the tree, no one knows how. Roots can store water as vapour on their surface against future shortage. Roots talk to funguses that carry messages to other trees. I become ever more aware of this busy interchange that lies under the stillness, and of how little of the complexity I understand. So I simply walk among the trees and admire them. They are aware of me, and I feel calm to be among them.

Oaks reach out in harmonious, fan-shaped patterns. Each species has a characteristic shape which we recognise in the leafless winter. The lime modestly covers its trunk in twigs and leaves, making an elegant oblong. The larch grows tall and slender. It is a pine that sheds its needles in the autumn, a little confused. I have an enormous ancient larch that has outgrown its racial memory. I suspect it is trying to become deciduous, but it is still a pine. Its branches wander in all directions aimlessly. It has lost its youthful slenderness and become a black-barked monster.

The final bitter irony is that we are conscious enough to realise that we cannot understand the complexities of our own bodies and the tree-covered planet we inhabit.

Having lived in this house for so long, I can measure fifty years' worth of growth. I live in the span of trees. The two-hundred-year-old oaks have scarcely stirred in that time – a limb or two lost, only one grandfather fallen – but I have outlived many a birch and alder. I have loved the trees planted by my predecessors, and I, in turn, have planted for the benefit of my successors. Planting an oak is making a toast to the future. I walk among the trees each day and they console me, yet I am an intruder, tolerated.

An admirable and well-meaning young man asked me (and many others) what we were doing to help save the planet from the depredations of global warming. He came to look me over, frowned at my old leaky house, but then he saw my trees, the ones I inherited and the fifteen thousand I have planted over forty years. I sent him this little ditty:

> How green are you? he asked.
> Does your roof leak heat?
> Your windows double-glazed?
> How big are your carbon feet?
> Do you drive, do you fly?
> Do you eat meat?
>
> I am old, more grey than green,
> No longer useful making things,
> Yet must confess, must own up,
> To meat and heat and car and plane.
>
> The greenest thing the old can do is die,
> But how in death to do it right?
> Should we ancients go en masse,
> Be buried and take up space,
> Or burn into greenhouse gas?
>
> Oh, I see you have a carbon sink,
> He said.
> They do have names, you know,
> Oak and Alder, Birch and Ash,

Larch and Beech, Thorn and Lime,
Hornbeam and Sally and Scots Pine,

All busily inhaling CO_2
Through wondrous photosynthesis,
And gifting us their oxygen,
Nature's own philanthropists.

I never heard back from him, but I set out to defend my trees to
the death – mine, not theirs.

The Twin Oak

My noble twin oak leans over the river,
As its branches reach for morning light,
For big bully brothers block the sun's rays
And shade the remains of the twin oak's day.
Its roots strain to hold that precarious weight
From a calamitous fall, sealing its fate.

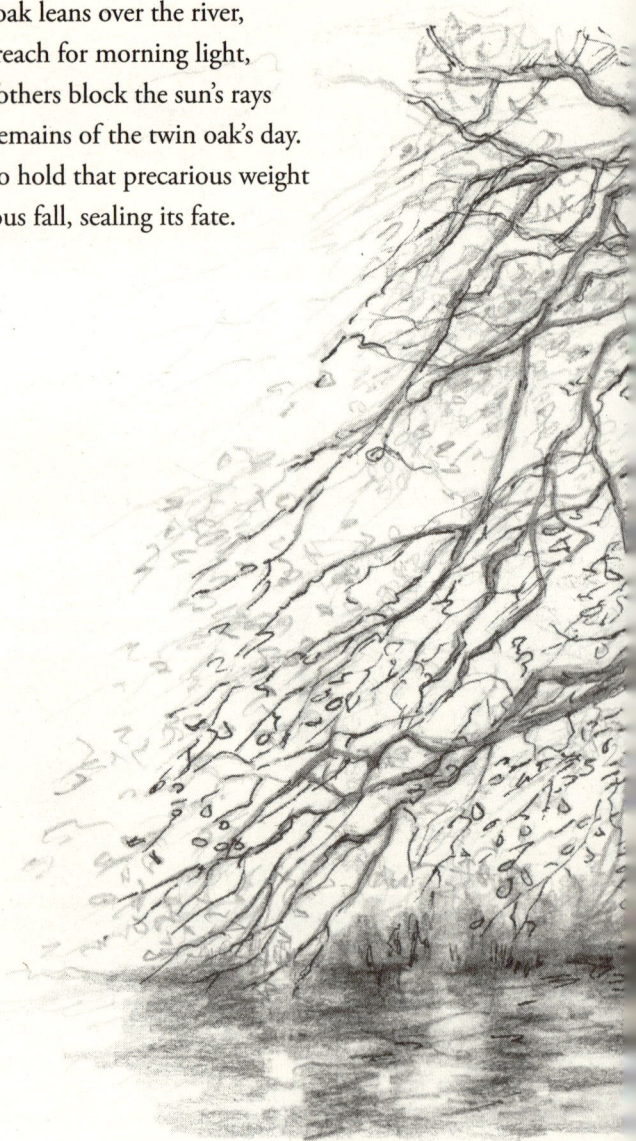

The Mighty Larch

Your normal larch is tall and slender,
But not sure if it is a pine or not,
For it sheds its needles in September.
Deciduously bemused,
Elegant, yes, but a little confused.

I have a larch that is out of hand.
Its hormones have let it down,
Forgot to tell it to stop growing.
It is even bigger than the oaks,
Its branches wander at will,
Blindly seeking destination.
A murky muddle of a tree,
But one much loved by me.

The Monkey Puzzle

So called because no monkey can
Figure out a climbing plan.
A tree so old it grew its spikes
To deter the dinosaur's appetite.
But our village sparks, Liam Sands,
He with no fingers on one hand,
Scaled it to the top each year
And covered it with fairy lights,
To every village child's delight.
How he did it he would not say
And took his secret to the grave.
Araucaria araucana,
To give it its proper name.
A noble Latin trope,
Not a silly monkey joke.

Lime Trees

We have a cluster of lime trees here,
A guard of honour up to the house.
Unter den Linden, you might say.

Modestly,
The limes clothe their trunks with leaves,
Making
Noble green oblongs of harmonious height.
In June
They burst into improbable bloom,
Hives erupt
And the roaring bees follow greedily on,
Feasting on those delicate white flowers.
Lime pollen is mildly narcotic to bees,
They often fall drunkenly out of the trees.

When Danny plunders his multiple hives,
The bees swarm over his bare arms
But never sting, they recognise,
The profound goodness of the man
And all the love he has for them.

'Dad!
Danny's here with the see-through honey.'
'Pellucid' is a better term, my son,
Scented Ambrosia, a promise of life never done.

But Danny ate it and is long since gone
And I will follow soon, but that boy,
The harbinger of honey,

Is now a battling lawyer,
And is (pro bono – no fees)
Intent on waging war
Against the slayers of the trees.

The Sally

The tenacious Sally is the Irish willow,
With a spreading paunch of a trunk.
One was planted or planted itself
Just outside my garden wall.
The swelling girth pushed down the wall.
'Cut it down,' a wise man urged,
But no, I rebuilt the wall with a curve.
That was twenty years ago
And now things are so much worse,
The monster is pushing at the curve.
I have had enough of this ugly beast.
'You can't cut it down,' they cried,
'It's the biggest Sally in the land,
A national treasure no less.
You must open your gates,
And share it with the common man.'

Scots Pine

Sparse limbs carve patterns in the sky,
Heroic roots grasp the poorest soil,
Ours is at the top of a hill.
A swing hangs from a branch so high,
Enough to make a child's toes coil,
Even as the landscape sways below.
'Higher' is the cry, or 'Let me down before I die.'
The other kids, waiting their turn, pass the time
Pelting pine nuts at the incumbent swinger.
Seven siblings sat this test
And took into the outer world
Fearless bravery,
Or a contempt for dad.

The Dying Sycamore

This sycamore was dying when I first got here,
That was forty-nine summers ago.
It was stunted, its bark cracked and sere.
I fed it nitrogen to make it grow,
But it shrivelled and wilted and branches fell.
But each spring it flaunts an umbrella of leaves,
That gains it another year's reprieve.
Too old for sex it no longer makes
Those helicopter seeds that litter the place.

When to Plant an Oak

When I'm losing my grip
And my feet won't touch the ground,
When all is lost, even hope,
Plant an oak.

When truth eludes me, and beauty flees,
Ask the trees,
Plant an oak.

When grief and loss tighten their grip,
Lean against an oak's great trunk
And ask it to take the pain away,
And promise as a way to pay
To
Plant an oak.

I used to set the table at a roar,
With applause ringing in my ears.
I forgot for years and years
To
Plant an oak

Like me, the oak cannot move and barely see,
Yet both begin to know how things work
And how to keep the world afloat.
Plant an oak.

As my life is coming to an end,

And I can barely walk or bend,
Yet I will kneel and scoop out earth,
And bring to birth,
An oak.

The Delicate Birch

One autumn day soft and still
I walked with Telsche to the court.
It was five all, we took a break.
Just above us was a young birch tree,
Its elegant branches looked Japanese.
And suddenly it caught a private breeze,
Trembled, and shook off all its leaves.
We smiled at it and then at each other,
A moment shared and cherished,
For as long or as short as we lived.

When she died, so very young,
We planted in her name
A Himalayan birch,
Now more than twenty years grown.
I can peel off its silver parchment bark
And write upon it a loving letter,
But to whom?

The Birch Arch

We planted young birch on both sides,
Now they reach up and join hands,
An avenue to walk under or ride,
Calming a mettlesome horse,
Settling a worried mind,
An arch of harmonious calm.

Tree Painting

Stripped of its cover of sensuous leaves,
Its beechwood home painted out,
It stands alone, nude, revealed,
Hanging there for all to see,
The intimate secrets of a tree.

How Mute

How mute the voice of Nature,
How silent the commands of trees,
Instructing the industrious leaf
To win carbon with such ease,
Telling its roots to send up sap.
Never a thank-you nor a please,
Only the rustling of its leaves.
For that mighty silent oak there
Is built only of water and air.

The Trees: A Requiem

Will they recall me, when I am gone,
A man who walked among them,
Who sought their wisdom,
Who wished them no harm?

He swore he would not die,
Until he figured out
How sap goes up a tree,
Defying gravity.
Alas,
He did not keep his oath,
But
Finally they gifted him
The mystery of the leaf,
On condition that it was
A secret he had to keep.

My land belonged to the Church of Ireland, and before that it was part of the monastic lands of Glendalough, the holiest place in Ireland. Before the monks, it was sacred to the Druids. I mark the movements of the season as they did, and by patient observance I hope to prise a secret or two from Nature's jealous grasp.

WINTER SOLSTICE

I have a walk-down well. Steps take you down so that you can fill your pail. The well is ancient and appears on the earliest Ordnance Survey maps. Over the years I have become aware that if I stand by the well at the winter solstice, I can watch the sun rise at the foot of the hill, and that its low arc follows exactly the arc of the hill. It skims over the treetops and sets with the dying year on the far side. I wonder if the Druids became aware of this alignment and sank a well to mark the spot, connecting sun to water.

We yearn to find meaning in Nature's implacable way, inventing religions, spilling blood, idolising, praying.

The new year has brought the stillness of snow. Nothing moves, except the black river, insisting on the primacy of flow. As I try to wrest answers from Nature's guarded secrets, I realise I am but a flea on the world's back, knowing only what I lack.

SHAMAN

Intellectually, I can accept that death is oblivion, yet it is impossible to grasp the concept of oblivion and to imagine the world without me in it, even though it managed to get along without me for a few millennia. As it was said, why do we fear the darkness to come, while we do not fear the darkness from which we came? My film *Zardoz*, set in the future, described a group of people who had found a way of eliminating death. They find eternal life unendurable. We are part of a world where all things pass and perish and are renewed with new life. To separate ourselves from this implacable law is to deny not only death, but life.

The tribe I lived with in the Amazon believed there was spirituality in everything, even locked in stone and in the flow of rivers. In trance, their animal familiars would help them connect with their ancestors and even witness the future, but especially to soar bird-like and travel freely across the cosmos. Bishop Berkeley taught that the external world can exist only as we perceive it through our five senses, yet in dream and trance we experience much without the aid of those senses. Jung claimed to have evidence of people dreaming of actual events that they themselves could not have witnessed, proving that there is an unconscious level where we are all connected. I love that possibility, but it has been rudely debunked by members of Jung's own profession. Nevertheless, he was an inspired poet of psychoanalysis, and his critics are prosaic mechanics.

Takuma, the shaman of the Kamayurá tribe in the Xingu, asked me what I did. I found it difficult to describe film to someone who had never seen one or watched television. When I told him it was possible to move freely from place to place, to go from close on a face to a wide shot of a landscape, to go back and forth in time and location, he nodded sagely and declared that I did the same work as he did.

FAMILY

Women

All my life I have lived among women. In the Second World War my father was away in the army and my mother was the head of the household. I had four aunts, but no uncles; two sisters and no brothers; I have had five daughters, but only two sons. I feel coarse in men's company and at ease with women. Yet most of my films have been about men, and I am often told by women that I know nothing about them. Surely, over three-quarters of a century of intimacy I must have picked up some insights into the feminine psyche.

'Like what?' Isabella asked.

'There are only two things I know for certain,' I said carefully. 'Women with curly hair would like to have straight hair, and women with straight hair would like to have curly hair.'

'What a condescending and belittling thing to say,' she said. 'And the other?'

'All women are searching for the perfect moisturiser.'

'There's some truth in that,' she allowed.

We were returning from a dinner party. I commented on the conversation and how impressed I was with one guest and his grasp of the body politic. She said, 'Did you see his wife wince when he started pontificating? He is a bully.' She went on to describe an emotional narrative that had run under the surface of the evening, which I had completely missed.

Katrine

Is Telsche's spirit soaring through the nether regions, alighting here and there, watching and laughing at our petty antics? How I would love to believe that, as her sisters do. Katrine was just a year and a week younger than Telsche. They were Irish twins, inseparable, a double act. Telsche was the anchor that allowed Katrine to fly, dance, be irrepressible, irresponsible. On Telsche's deathbed, Katrine promised to be a mother to Daphne, Telsche's seven-year-old daughter, and she has tried to be one. But more than that, in my absence with a second family she became the centre, taking care of her mother and her siblings, as well as Daphne, to my shame.

She has written a funny and moving account of the hours following Telsche's death, in the form of a film script that she wants to direct. She first needed to learn, to get experience, to make something she could show publicly, to earn the confidence of financiers. Her idea was to make a documentary about her father, who would give a masterclass as she went along. We have been doing that – on and off – for the last three years. I asked her when she was planning to finish it. 'Never,' she said. 'I'd like to go on making it for ever.' It has been painful and joyful, and I have passed on to her a little of what I know about life and family and movie-making. She lived in the happy shadow of her sister but has now become a powerful force. She is a wickedly funny mimic and raconteur.

Her documentary found its way to the Cannes Film Festival and into people's homes. While acknowledging its virtues, I am acutely embarrassed when I am obliged to watch it.

Christel

My first wife, Christel, would leap out of bed the moment she woke up. She exploded into the day. When she decided to clean our small apartment, she would wash everything – clothes, dishes, shelves, curtains, windows. She would chivvy me to strip off so she could wash my shirt and underwear. Finally, her own clothes would go in and she would finish by scrubbing the floor, naked.

She came from a small farm in northern Germany. It had been in the family for generations. They grew cabbages for sauerkraut. The threat of the bank foreclosing on the farm was constant. Consequently, she had a fear of official letters and refused to open them. For her, money was entirely emotional. When she wanted it, I would ask her how much she needed. 'Just give me loads of it,' she would reply.

We travelled the world making movies, and she measured all the people she encountered against the inhabitants of her small home town of Wesselburen. I have to say it worked rather well. She was a shrewd judge of character, much better than I. I had fallen in love with her vitality and her foreignness, but critically when I met her she was broken-hearted after the end of a long, passionate love affair. She was brash and abrasive. If she felt out of her depth in a conversation, she would disrupt it. We fought constantly. She embarrassed me in front of my intellectual colleagues from the BBC. Looking back, I can see she was often puncturing their pomposity. She demanded my attention and felt threatened by the clever women I encountered in my work.

We were dining at Mr Chow's in Knightsbridge with Tony Woollard and his wife, Joan. Tony was the production designer of *Leo the Last*, which we had been shooting for eight weeks.

It was Saturday night, the end of an exhausting week. I could hardly eat from tiredness. Inevitably, we talked shop, excluding Christel. (At dinner during a shoot John Ford wisely forbade anyone to mention the movie being worked on.) She responded by clattering into the conversation and making it impossible to finish a sentence. She had been starved of my attention for two months and more, and she was determined to claim it back. Finally, I snapped.

'Come on. We're leaving,' I said.

'I'm not leaving. I haven't finished my dinner.'

I got up, took her hand and attempted to pull her to her feet. She would not budge. I tried again. She sat tight. I heard myself shouting, as though from far away. Silence fell over the raucous tables. Enraged, I gave her a mighty pull just at the moment when she had decided to get up of her own volition. She flew over my shoulder. We were upstairs next to the spiral staircase, and she tumbled down it. I dashed after her, picked her up at the bottom and dragged her out of the restaurant. There was a cab waiting outside – in the way that only happens in the movies – and I bundled her into it.

We sat in silence, side by side. Gloomily, I felt this was finally the end of the troubled marriage. There could be no way back from here. The silence lengthened. She turned her head towards me. I was surprised to see that her eyes were shining.

'You were magnificent,' she said. 'As I was falling, I saw all those women's eyes watching and wishing they had a man who cared enough about them to throw them down the stairs.'

The late, great Hollywood agent Bobby Littman witnessed all this. He came over to the Woollards and asked to be allowed to pick up the tab. 'I'll put it down to entertainment,' he said. Next day he sent Christel flowers, with a note saying, 'Love takes many forms.'

Forty years later, our marriage long over, I would still see her frequently, and I was always reminded of how well I loved her and how glad I was that I no longer lived with her. She felt exactly the same way. We would sip tea together and wonder what all the '*Sturm und Drang*' was about.

At the end, no longer able to spring out of bed, she remained in it and received visitors regally. She never complained or lost her love of life. Charley's twin, Daisy, took care of her in those declining years.

Summoned to the hospital where she lay dying, I sat by her side. I spoke to her of our years together, of our children, but she was unconscious. I pressed her hand, but there was no response. Her breathing became more and more shallow. It was impossible to define the exact moment when it stopped. The great spirit had left. I was sitting next to a stranger.

It was some hours before Charley, Katrine and Daisy were able to get there, and as I stayed by her side awaiting them, my mind wandered over the times we had shared. I recalled my first sight of her – flashing eyes, the lustrous skin, the wild spirit – at that Beethoven concert.

Katrine was touched that I, the man her mother loved, had been with her when she died. As she recounted the story to her friends, holding her hand soon became 'she died in Dad's arms'.

We buried her in Paris, next to Telsche. That was her wish. At the graveside I saluted her courage. When I had told her that I intended to leave the safety of the BBC and take my chances making movies, she had never shown any anxiety. We had four young children and went off to Hollywood, later heading to the South Pacific to make *Hell in the Pacific* with Lee Marvin and Toshiro Mifune. She and the children came along, as they did to the Amazon and the river featured in *Deliverance*.

Lola

At seventeen, Lola, the eldest of the second litter, takes her studies seriously, works diligently, edits the school magazine, wants to go to college in America. I suspect she needs to get away from all of us, and this is the only course she knows.

> My Lola Loo is seventeen,
> Building her own citadel.
> In her shuttered eyes,
> I glimpse the climbing walls,
> No trumpet of mine will bring down her Jericho.
>
> Her mobile pings and her thumbs tap out retorts.
> She smiles into her phone,
> But facing me the portcullis slams shut.
> My storming love bounces back,
> From her stony stare.
>
> Unbidden she cleaned my kitchen.
> It shines with spick and span,
> My clutter black-bagged,
> Hurled from the parapets.

Why does it feel like a hostile act?
Because I can't find anything,
Especially the corkscrew.
It must be in the moat.

Five years later, I witness her graduation ceremony at Trinity College, Dublin. She gains a First in English and receives the rarely given Gold Medal for her work. Samuel Beckett was one of the few to get the medal before her. The borrowed robes look tatty and the silly hat does not fit. The medal has an image of Elizabeth I, who founded the college.

We have breakfast together before the event. She takes lunch after it with her mother and Adrian, keeping her parents close but apart. Her studies have brought us together. She says one of the reasons she wanted to study literature was to get closer to me. When she left school, I bought her a Kindle and stuffed it with all my favourite novels. Now I follow her into places I have not ventured before. I could never manage Virginia Woolf, but Lola taught me how to read *To the Lighthouse*, how it progresses like our thought processes, how the events and notions occupy a single day but tell the story of a family. The lack of narrative drive defeated me in a way that *Ulysses* did not. *Ulysses* was a journey through a single day, whereas *To the Lighthouse* has the stasis of a single room. Helped as I was by Lola's guidance, I grasped it at last, and I have to confess that I found the Ramsay family's return to their holiday house, left empty during the First World War, hugely rewarding. Oh, the power of narrative. Time had passed, things had changed. Story.

Lola then does her master's at Cambridge. Her focus is narrowed down to the short stories of Lydia Davis, who was formerly married to Paul Auster. Lydia and Paul studied Beckett in Paris together, and you can detect his severe influence on Paul's novels and Lydia's stories. We all fell in love with Paul's *New York Trilogy*, but one of his recent books consisted solely of descriptions of all the apartments he had occupied in his life. It reminded me of the French artist, Claude Lazar, who paints empty rooms. Some of Paul's rooms were also occupied by Lydia, but she is not mentioned by name. Paul is now married to the author Siri Hustvedt. If the cliché 'tall dark and handsome' was waiting for Paul to fulfil it, so Siri is 'tall, blonde and beautiful'. What a startling pair they make. I suspect from her work that Lydia is petite.

Siri's early work appeared to be aping Paul's, but it is now so powerful and original. Paul can be found lurking in Lydia's stories. Lately, when I see him he looks haunted, like an escapee from one of his novels.

In 2017 Paul startles us by writing a nine-hundred-page novel, *4 3 2 1*. It is the story of his life, and how different it could have been had he taken certain choices at particular points, and we are treated to four possible Pauls. It is intimidating. I can barely lift it. Siri trumps him with an even longer book. Forests have been felled.

Lola is now deep into her PhD. Her subject is punctuation. In the distant past words simply tumbled together. An Irish monk came up with the idea of punching a hole in the vellum between the words, hence the term 'punctuation'. How could I have survived eighty years without knowing that? By keeping pace with Lola, I experience vicariously the education I never had.

Lee

My son Lee is fourteen and just recovered from a collarbone broken on the rugby pitch. He plays with a fierce, passionate grace. His speed and guile weave him a path between defenders and he floats for the line, comes to earth and touches down. His tongue is as quick as his feet. He spins, tests, provokes; he pushes the limits of tolerance in parents and teachers. He is a sporting hero, and so has the air of a conqueror. Will he be a stand-up comedian, street trader, con man or politician? He calls me Johnny Boy, and even in affectionate jest it borders on disrespect.

He skips backwards in front of me with urgent gestures.

'Dad, I need a hundred euro.'

'What for?'

'It doesn't matter. I really need it.'

'I'm not going to give you a hundred euro,' I say indignantly, and walk on. He gestures with his hands that I should calm down. He smiles to placate, going easy on me.

'OK, Johnny Boy, I'll take seventy-five.'

I am incensed. 'No. I am not giving you seventy-five euro.'

My anger sobers him and he walks silently by my side for a while. Then he speaks in a quiet, steady voice.

'Dad, I'll take fifty. That's my last offer.'

His early intent was to kill the Japanese whale hunters, but his ambition has broadened. He wants to change the world, as any decent boy would. To this end he has joined the Socialist Workers Party and is now studying at King's College, London – philosophy, politics and law, window dressing for a law degree.

He recently spent a couple of summer weeks with me. He loves the land and would run down to the river each morning and swim with his black Alsatian. We ate dinner together each night, and I discovered him as an adult. We talked politics, art and trees, but mostly about family: of the break-up of my marriage to his mother; of his two sisters, and his brother and sisters from my first litter. Going into his final year at law school he is also a cage fighter.

Lili Mae

If Lola has her academic prowess, and Lee was the lord of the playing field, then Lili Mae at eleven had no need of either. School work held no terrors for her. She worked methodically and steadily. When she came up to visit me, she filed all the clutter on my desk. Her discipline was ballet. Her beguiling smile and gentle charm paved her path to the future and she walked it with grace and humour. She cares about her family, all of us, and regards us, I suspect, as a bunch of errant adolescents whom she tolerates and treats with indulgence.

At seventeen she decided she wanted to study classics. 'But they don't teach Latin in your school, let alone Greek,' I said.

'I think I can pick it up on my own,' she said.

Now eighteen, she is reading philosophy at Edinburgh.

Charley

In contrast to all this academic success, my son Charley suffers from acute dyslexia. Special schools and private tutoring all failed to teach him to read. When he was seventeen, I took him off to the Amazon rainforest to play a leading role in *The Emerald Forest*. Before that he was the Young Mordred in *Excalibur*.

He tried to follow an acting career, but when asked to read a scene at auditions, he would be unable to do so. He developed a fear of the process.

He has found a niche, riding his motorbike around the world making TV adventure series. Technology has come to his aid. He is able to dictate emails into his iPhone. He is the author of three books chronicling his adventures, all written by dictation. I said, 'Charley, I know you can't write your books, but do you read them?'

'You know I can't,' he said, 'but a lot more people read my books than read yours.'

I had to admit to the truth of that.

He had a bad crash on his motorbike in 2015. An ankle and a wrist broken, a shin bone shattered. This man of action was forced to lie inert for months. I urged him to write his story. I said, 'Charley, as you were flying through the air at sixty miles per hour towards a brick wall, your life flashes before you, and you are back as a child in Annamoe . . .'

The book is just out and has sold 20,000 copies of the hardback in the first month.

Daisy

Charley has a twin sister, Daisy. Born minutes apart, they are so different that they make a mockery of horoscopes. They are chalk and cheese. She came out second, a breech baby. If you enter the world feet first, you see things differently. Charley was always comfortable in his skin, whereas Daisy was perplexed and astonished by her surroundings. She felt like an alien on this planet.

When they were little, Daisy looked out for Charley and protected him from the many hazards awaiting him, of which he was blissfully unaware. When she was four, I heard her asking a girl if she was a twin. The girl was not. 'It must be sad to be alone in the world,' said Daisy. Later, if Charley had a girlfriend, Daisy would become her best friend. She would relieve Charley of the wooing process.

She is always studying, trying to make sense of things. When her mother got sick, Daisy found her vocation. She cared for Christel for several years until her death. Daisy pushed that wheelchair all over London. They argued a lot, interrupted each other and shouted each other down, and were deeply devoted. In some ways Daisy took up the role I had abandoned. She is kind and loving and loyal and grieves for her mother.

You can't cast your children. You get what you are sent. The genes are shaken up and out they come. When we had our first child, Telsche, I developed a theory of how to raise children. When the second arrived, I found I had to modify the theory. By the third and fourth I abandoned all theory and played it by the seat of my pants.

Same with actors. Theories don't work. They all need something different, but like children, they all need love. Lee Marvin advised me that all you need to deal with actors is a whip and a chair. Certainly, demand everything they have to give, but holding them off does not work. Hold them close.

My children all appear to have weathered the break-up of their parents' marriage in their different ways.

A LOVE STORY

Wives gone, children grown, he lived alone, finding consolation in solitude, seeking peace of mind. They met by chance. He remembered her as a child. Their families had been neighbours.

Between them they pieced together a shared past – sunlit, golden, tragic. Her father had been killed when she was nine. She had become a beautiful woman. They went to an exhibition, then lunch at the Tate. He told her about his life and losses as he had told no other. They fell in love. He felt unworthy of a love so freely given and saw how foolish he must look in the eyes of the world, yet they enjoyed being together and were disconsolate apart.

Love is sacred to her. It cannot be challenged or explained. It just is. She took his heart. Her love burned him.

Years passed, and their bond grew stronger. Their need to be together grew ever more important.

Her light shines on the world. Striding through the park, her feet scarcely touch the ground. She rejoices in a cavorting child, finds beauty beneath the carapace of a tottering old lady. Her eyes smile on the morning, and the day smiles back. She can conjure the sun from the clouds. She is brimming with health and bursting with a soaring spirit. Her laughing green eyes sweep the world and offer benediction to all.

Cigarette

There were plans, even bookings, to go to other Parisian restaurants, but they often found themselves drifting back to Ma Bourgogne, not just because it was close to the hotel, and not only because of its famous steak tartare, but because they enjoyed the mocking waiters and the ambience of charade.

The head waiter had a benign air of superiority and treated their choices with amused ridicule. The woman had an open face and dancing green eyes that invited contact. The man was much older, could have been her father, yet they seemed very involved in one another, very much at ease; if it weren't for the disparity in their ages, they might even be lovers. They took a lot of wine, she more than he. She had an insatiable thirst for life and drank it prodigiously. The waiters were drawn to her, circled the table in attendance, but always with a sense of parody.

They were back, without a reservation. The head waiter held up his hands, as though to ward off the devil. Not you again. He indicated the occupied tables with an elegant sweep of his arm. He took a certain pleasure in sending them away, but her eyes melted him. She was life and could not be denied. He sighed. He gave instructions to a waiter and shunted them off to a corner by the bar where there were just two tables hidden from the main dining room. It was a narrow space, and they sat side by side. The other table was occupied by two couples, friends, it seemed, of the *patron*, who perched over them at the bar.

The waiter reappeared with the specials written on a blackboard that he rested on their table, with his face smiling over its top. She felt hemmed in by it. She wanted steak tartare, but the waiter shook his head and pointed to the steak au poivre like a teacher looking for the right answer from a straying pupil. She conceded. He left.

'I think we're in the winners' enclosure,' she said, watching the *patron* indulging his friends. The man laughed. He loved the way wit defined her world. The intimacy of the hidden space matched their mood, and sins were confessed and forgiven. He made a biblical reference, and she admitted that she had never read the Bible. He was shocked. It was so woven into Western culture that you had to know something of it. 'Then teach me,' she said. He started with 'In the beginning was the Word and the Word was made Flesh.' So beautiful, the King James version, but the modern translations are mundane and disappointing. He made a joke about holy ghostwriters. She had a look of longing, as though hungry for his knowledge, and it encouraged him and he started on Moses, but he realised that she was looking not at him but past him to the *patron*, and not even at him, but at the packet of Marlboro Reds in his hand, and she saw that, covertly and illegally, he was smoking one of them.

'May I have one?' she cried, brushing Moses aside. The *patron* stubbed out his cigarette and brusquely refused her. Not allowed. Against the law.

She turned back to the man. Would he please tell her about turning water into wine? He noticed that although their water glasses were full, the wine glasses were empty.

More wine was brought in the conventional manner. It was at a wedding, he said, the only reference to marriage in the New Testament.

They looked up. The *patron* was looming over them, the Marlboro Reds packet pointing at them like a gun. She gave a gasp of surprise and took one. At arm's length, he flicked his lighter at her. The two couples at the next table watched carefully, then lit up too, all four of them.

'Will you buy me a Bible?' she said, inhaling down to her toes.

She is awash in emotions. They come in waves and crash over her, rendering her helpless in the face of their power, every one a tsunami. There is a purity about this, an honesty. She is washed clean.

Her insults have a dated quality, probably learnt from her American grandfather. She calls him a jackass and tells him to 'get a grip'. Her love is unswerving and keeps me afloat. Her name is Hope, and hope was her gift to me. I have known her all her life, but we fell in love when she was thirty-seven and I seventy-three, a pleasing symmetry, but a wide gap in age to broach.

She is a walker. There is no illness she cannot walk away from, and no problem she cannot solve by the time she reaches her destination. I worship the ground she walks so lightly upon.

Love

The successes and failures, the stresses and struggles are the broken toys of time. What remains are the moments of shared joy with those we love, of enlightened understanding between friends, affection between colleagues, of love given and received in all its forms, the aching love of children, the intimate love of lovers, and the grief of love lost as those we love are picked off one by one by the relentless cruelty of death.

THE MOVIES

Films have been my life, ruling it, and in some sense, ruining it. I have been at their beck and call, always waiting, never able to make plans. My begging bowl has been held out for the money to make them. I have wheedled actors, flattered financiers, lied about my intentions and concealed my artistic ambitions, and audiences have often rejected the final result. I have spent more time on films I have not made than on the ones I have, because there are many reasons why a film should not be made.

For the fortieth anniversary of the Cannes Film Festival, it was decided to give a special award to admired directors. Billy Wilder and I were the first to arrive for the rehearsal. The woman in charge, nervous at the prospect of corralling so many luminaries, fluttered up to us and asked if we would mind waiting until the others arrived. 'Do I mind waiting?' said Billy. 'I've spent my life waiting – waiting for the money, waiting for the actors to read the script, waiting for the cameraman, waiting for the sun to come out, waiting for it to go in. I made two movies with Marilyn Monroe. Do I mind waiting? In fifty years of film-making, do you know how long the camera was running? Maybe two weeks.'

In some ways, film was at its purest in the early silent era. Everything that has been added since – speech, colour, stereo, CGI, 3D – has also taken something away. The attempt to approximate life is futile. Film is not life and never can be. It is much closer to dreaming than waking. The mainstream movie of today comes with exaggerated sound effects, heavily amplified music and fast editing. It is overloaded with information and bludgeons the audience into submission. Huge audiences respond to this visual and auditory overload and derive visceral and sensual excitement from its offerings, but each new picture has to top its predecessor for spectacular special effects. The law of diminishing returns comes into play. Now that people know the computer can manipulate everything they are no longer impressed. A cynicism has set in, and an exhaustion.

Black-and-white film invited us into a contiguous world, recognisable but as different from life as dreams. A black-and-white still portrait can often be more revealing than one in colour, because it strips away a layer and finds what lies beneath. I made *The General* in black and white and faced huge prejudice and resistance from both distributors and the public. There is no going back, so serious film-makers desaturate the colour or work with a narrow palette to approximate black and white by subterfuge.

A good director will expunge everything that is inessential and include only what is vital to their purpose. Their compositions will lead the eye to what is central. These processes lend a film power. If, when watching a movie, one comes to realise that everything in every frame is intended, the heart sings.

Ben Wheatley has said his astonishing movie *High-Rise* was influenced by *Zardoz*, and that the Holy Trinity of British film are John Boorman, Nic Roeg and Ken Russell. It is a generational thing. My British trinity would have been Carol Reed, Michael Powell and David Lean. Only by standing on their shoulders could we see our future films. Then we looked to learn from further afield. We waited impatiently to see the latest Bergman, Visconti, Fellini, Ozu, Kurosawa or Truffaut in art houses that have long since gone. In the American mainstream, Hitchcock was in his pomp and John Ford bestrode the range. With no videos or DVDs, we had to get out there and stand in line, relishing the anticipation of the queue.

The mystique of movies has been lost as people watch them on their laptops and mobile phones. The very first films by the Lumière brothers were ninety seconds long. I notice that the videos posted on YouTube are mostly of that length. We've gone full circle. Why should films be two hours long? Yet because movies are so available, they are often watched over and over.

Well, as it happens, the two-hour movie is being usurped by the long, high-quality TV series, financed by American cable companies like HBO. *The Sopranos*, *Mad Men* and *Game of Thrones* sprawl over endless episodes, continuing until their makers collapse from exhaustion. Movie writers and directors, frustrated by the crassness of the Hollywood studios, are increasingly drawn to this form.

Movies are always seeking endings that grow out of the body of the story, that are earned and satisfying, whereas the series is searching for material that will let it continue. It must avoid endings at all costs. Of course, it needs climaxes, but the climaxes must lead to further developments, not conclusions.

The audience come to know the characters, identify with their problems and enjoy their successes. These are friends, and we need our friends to stay with us. Even though these long-form series are well financed, their length requires that they be shot faster than movies, typically ten minutes of footage a day rather than the three minutes a day for a feature film. To achieve this, the scripts must be dialogue-heavy, since talky scenes can be shot more quickly than action or dialogue scenes with complex designs. The lighting and camera movements must be simpler. Scenes shot in tight close-up relieve the DP of lighting big sets. The cameramen are instructed to shoot 'flat' with multiple cameras, with the atmosphere put in in post-production. Actors work in front of green screens, with the landscapes and city streets matted on in post-production. Most of them prefer longer scenes containing more lines that they can get their teeth into. The meticulous nature of shooting a feature film is taxing for actors, and they can find it difficult to keep up their energy levels as it is pieced together fragment by fragment.

The feature film is a director's medium; the TV series is usually dictated by a producer or, as they are now called, a show runner. They plan, instruct a team of writers and hire the several directors they will need. It is a complex operation requiring contributions from many hands. I find the results tedious, the obligation to watch a chore.

It seems that story-telling is essential to the human condition, and it has passed through many forms, from the Minnesingers to *Game of Thrones*. Stories aim to give meaning to a world manifestly lacking it. Making up stories means having a licence to lie but an obligation to truth. Looking back, I regret that too often my lies have concealed the truth rather than revealing it. I have been cowardly in life but brave in my film-making. I have been a better person exercising my craft and a lesser man living my life.

I came home from a school cricket match, and my father asked me how I had fared. I had been bowled for a duck. I knew how much it meant to him, so I invented an innings. I described the various shots I had made and the runs scored. It was vivid and convincing. My stories were so much more real than the messy reality. He questioned me closely as to the details, then told me he had watched the match and witnessed my abject failure. The humiliation should have cured me of lying, but it did not. He desperately wanted me to succeed as a cricketer, where he had failed, but jealous of my mother's love for me he also wanted me to fail. His relish in catching me out made me hate him. It was only when our roles were reversed and I was taking care of him that we became friends.

THE END AND THE ENDING OF LIFE

As I approach the end of my life, I contemplate choosing the moment to end it. Suicide by the young is abhorrent, but old people should be allowed to choose the time of their demise. No one should have to endure years of mental and physical decline, dependence, humiliation, incontinence and pain; this is the future I must expect. My long-life genes and vigorous immune system are programmed to keep me alive despite my decline – failing eyesight, hearing loss, peripheral neuropathy. I walk with a stick. The wheelchair beckons. Currently, I am still able to prepare and cook my meals, pay my bills, get up and down the stairs, but for how long? My daughter Daisy is preparing a flat for me in her little house in Fulham. She wants to care for me as she cared for her mother. I appreciate her kindness but find the prospect stifling. The National Health Service spends 70 per cent of its resources on people in the last two years of their lives. Doctors are dedicated to patching them up and keeping them going.

Why should so many suffer years of agony and not be allowed to gracefully choose the time of their exit? Old believers, lingering on, would often say, 'I think God has forgotten me.'

But how to make an elegant, bloodless, noiseless exit that does not dismay my children?

Maybe Tomorrow

July 2017. As old men do, I fall and break my right femur.

I lie on the kitchen floor, my supper in pan and oven. I had promised never to be without my phone, but just this once it is on the far side of the kitchen table. I move and pain leaps at me. I weigh my options. It's Friday evening. No one will come by the house until Mary at 9 a.m. on Monday morning. Three nights. A cold lingering death.

I inch my way across the floor towards the table, leaving a stain of pain like the sticky wake of a snail. My arms drag the broken body up the north face of the table. I can see the phone but pass out for a moment. Is this the exit, like it or not? I come to and feel peace. Unbidden, my arm reaches out and clutches the phone. Supper is up in smoke and filling the kitchen. A wave of pain swamps me. Help!

Ambulance, stretcher, hospital. From independence to total dependence.

I am in a queue of stretchers. We are strapped in tight. We inch towards the surgeon. Blood pressure. What is your name and date of birth? Does it match the wristband?

'Eighteenth of January, 1933. Hitler has just come to power.'

They must have made a bad mistake somewhere down the line. A mark is placed on my thigh where the knife will be inserted. My stretcher is moved closer to the surgeon. He has fifteen cases to get through, I am told. An epidural converts my lower body into an alien statue. I tap it with my finger. I watch the surgeon, Mr Murphy, digging and probing in my thigh, but feel nothing.

I am wheeled into recovery. Excruciating pain all down my right leg. If anyone brushes the skin, I hit the roof. Spasms shoot up the wounded limb. I cry out.

Next morning the cruel physio gets me out of bed and makes me walk, clutching a Zimmer frame. My leg muscles have amnesia. I marvel that people walk carelessly on their hind legs.

I am moved to the Royal Hospital, Donnybrook, which is

dedicated to rehab. Erica is a strong, finely balanced woman. She is everything we, her charges, are not, but she is intent on mending these broken old men. The exercises are painful and exhausting, but surprisingly exhilarating. Can I be a boy again and jump over walls? No, you never will. *You are old, Father William.* But, Erica says, 'Our claim is that everyone walks out of here.'

I am in love with her, so I work hard to please her. My leg regains a vague memory of its function, but the knee cap pops out and won't support me.

At breakfast I study the grey faces at the table as they eat their porridge. Our pills are dished out, drugs that keep us alive. We are living much longer but spending those extra years like this. Extended old age is the penalty we pay for living a healthy life, someone said.

My children respond to my plight with a rush of concern and love. I lie there helpless, and they compete to supply that help. I am humbled.

Lola does a week and takes charge, fixing things up, then Lili takes over. She comes every day.

Daisy sails in for a week, showering me with concern and health foods. Her generous heart has found a perch. The following week brings her twin, Charley, just recovered from his crippling motorbike crash and now promoting the book it inspired. The nurses flutter about him.

Lee arrives next, heavily muscled, hot from his cage-fighting and law studies. He goes up to the house and fits it up for a returning cripple.

Hope brings a wave of love but is furious with me for falling. She fears I have resigned from life.

Katrine takes the last week, conjuring up great lunches at my house, tempting me home. Then I run out of children, but Lili lives nearby and comes in every day, steadfast. She is slight, with white skin and mahogany hair, a ballerina. In a few days she will go to Edinburgh to study philosophy. I am loath to lose her.

I am reading *Homo Deus*, Yuval Noah Harari's sequel to *Sapiens*. I find a passage in which he warns us not to expect wisdom from old men. Their minds are decaying like their bodies. I read this out to Lili Mae. She says that explains why we are not doing so well with the crossword.

I am given an intelligence test to see if I am sufficiently compos mentis to be allowed home. I am taken to a kitchen and challenged to make my breakfast. I pass these tests by the skin of my teeth. So, after seven weeks, I am home, though not walking out of there unaided – I need a Zimmer. I inhale the fifteen thousand trees that enclose me and the centre holds.

My good friend Garech, he who wished he had never been born, told me on the phone that he wanted to die, he just wanted to die. I hurried down to Luggala, past the aching majesty of its lake lying in its fold of hills, and found him in bed, still wishing to die. I said, 'I can help you, Garech. I will put a pillow over your face. It will all be over in five minutes.'

He abandoned his mantra of yearning for death and fell silent. I picked up a pillow and plumped it up.

'I don't want to die today,' he said at last.

However despairing we are, we don't want to die today. Maybe tomorrow.

Alas, in 2018 he shocked us all by declaring that he was broke and obliged to sell his five thousand acres, his lake and his exquisite Gothic house. I understood at last his cry for death, and I felt ashamed of my frivolous response. He was reeling from an earlier blow, when his lover of seventeen years, Susan, left him, worn out by his drinking. He went off to Singapore for his annual visit to his wife, Princess Purna. From there he wrote Susan a letter, which she said was so beautiful that she burst into tears. She relented.

He has just got back to London, where Susan lives, and they were due to have lunch today, Sunday 11 March 2018, but dear Garech died yesterday of a massive heart attack. He and Luggala were such a part of my life and the lives of my children that it feels like an ending. He once said, 'Luggala made me, and I, in part, made it.' When he lost Luggala, he lost his life. He was fatally wounded without it.

Gone are the lavish entertainments, the parties, the poets and the pipers and the fragile Garech making a haven against the cruel world.

THE UNIVERSE

On Hollywood contracts these days you are required to cede to the studio rights to all the territories in the world and the universe, in case some new planet is discovered where they can sell your movie. Roger Corman tells me, 'I always say to them, "You can have the world, but I am keeping the universe."'

What is the purpose of this universe of billions of stars hurtling through space at breakneck speed? And what is this 'space' they pass through? An absence? How much of it is there, this space? Is it infinite? An infinity of absence? We cannot get our heads around the notion of infinity. And what was all this space up to before the Big Bang? Just hanging about, waiting profoundly?

These stars are just continuously exploding hydrogen bombs. Some of them have planets. The theory is that there must be billions of planets, all varying in size, temperature and atmosphere. Eventually, Chance will come up with one that is furnished with the conditions for life, and it turns out it was ours. Earth is poorly named. It is mostly water. Where did it come from? The other planets that circle the sun don't seem to have any, or maybe just a puddle or two.

Our little planet revolves around a star on the edge of an unremarkable galaxy. After millions of years of trying, of trial and error, Chance produces thousands of beautiful and grotesque creatures. These species are programmed to fight for survival and to reproduce themselves. In order to do so, they need to kill and eat other species. Eventually, Chance, the great creator, comes up with *Homo sapiens*, a species that destroys, dominates and eats other species. Once this is achieved, it sets about torturing and murdering its own. Those that survive these horrors will eventually die. Every creature that is born will die. This is the situation we face as we enter the world. Our psychology allows us to ignore or deny this fate, though consciousness will nag away at us with the mortal truth. This random chaos is sternly controlled by mathematical laws that come from we know not where. Mathematics is not invented but discovered. Exceptions to its rules are subatomic particles that act like unruly children, passing through buildings, disappearing, being in two places at once; but when they grow up to be atoms and molecules, they have to obey the laws.

There are some who believe that synchronicity and coincidence are leaks from an underlying pattern that quietly makes sense of it all, but this is just a grasping of cosmic straws.

I am paying a fleeting visit to this planet, during which I make and tell stories about life as I find it. Our stories attempt to find meaning, something absent in the account of life set out above. I have witnessed the wonders and horrors around me, but no meaning presents itself. Yet the human body is immensely complex, as though designed to house creatures more brilliant than us. I often feel like a dim lodger who does not understand the house rules. But it is our modest essence, our core, our spirit that animates these amazing machines.

The universe is profligate, excessive, a vast release of energy with no destination or purpose. It will eventually burn out and expire.

Meanwhile, on a calm, balmy day I sit peacefully on a deckchair watching my trees grow. The reality is that I am travelling around the sun at thirty kilometres per second and our galaxy is hurtling through space. We are gifted illusions, soon to be superseded by robots, a species that will not be subject to disease and death nor the need to sleep. Their superior intelligence will be discouraging to us. Giving some thought to the advent of a robotic world, I wrote a radio play that attempts to chart the way our two species might relate to each other. It raises the issue of love and whether it will be possible or useful for robots to experience it.

If they are to succeed us, their lives will be arid without it. Will they step into our bodies as we vacate them?

CONCLUSIONS

The title of this book promises conclusions, yet I have offered few so far. *Confusions* might have been a better title, or even *Confessions*. Well, here are a few that might help if you are thinking of making movies.

– It is vital to make plans. It is futile to make plans. The world is ruled by chance. Take your chances.

– While it is right to celebrate the weird wonder that is each moment of life, inspiration usually comes out of the boredom of 'dull quarters of an hour'.

– Take your work seriously, and not seriously at all. That is a balance few achieve. More often we veer towards the two extremes of earnestness and flippancy. Earnestness makes you a bore. Flippancy renders you impotent.

– If you are not dismayed by your ignorance, you have learnt nothing. Wisdom is not minding not knowing.

– In old age, our world shrinks. Only love can expand to include more and many, especially actors. Compassion allows us to embrace more still, even the awkward actors.

– Doubts are more valuable than opinions. People who define themselves by a set of opinions feel threatened by doubts. Doubting is acknowledging complexity. However, if you can see several ways of shooting a scene, you can end up not making a decision – fatal.

– There is something absurd about taking this business of movie-making seriously, sweating blood to make something so ephemeral. I once described movie-making as inventing impossible problems and failing to solve them. This may have been God's problem with the universe. Yet it is the absurd that best describes our dance with chance as we dash through life, leaving 'the rags of time' in our wake.

FURTHER THOUGHTS WHILE WATCHING
MY TREES GROW

Ours is a tree planet. When there are more people than trees, it will all be over.

The west of Ireland is bereft of trees. 'Not a tree to hang a man from, not a foot of earth to bury him in,' complained Cromwell. But if you plant them, they will make soil.

The great forests of the world, in order of magnitude, are in the Amazon, Borneo, Northern Australia, the Congo, China. There are many more smaller ones. If you cut them down, the rain stops falling and they turn into desert.

When we were filming *The Emerald Forest*, we were based for a month in Belém, at the mouth of the Amazon. The forest there grows on sand. Over thousands of years the trees have built a layer of soil. Cut them down, and you're back to sand.

In a rainforest the action is in the canopy, 300 feet above. All the air space is taken. It is dark and gloomy below. Nasty vegetation that lives on the detritus of the trees stings you, injects your skin with venom, rips your clothes, even bites you. Up in the canopy is glorious profusion. In the town of Belém is an ice-cream parlour that advertises 'Forty Forest Flavours' – infinite diversity from the sun and water.

The history of the world is the story of clearing the forests to grow food and graze cattle. To reverse that momentum is hard. We will have to reform our relationship with the trees and the soil.

Most people around the world are worried about where their next meal is coming from. Only by giving massive aid to poor countries can we check migration – and the cutting down of trees. Put simply, we need more trees and fewer people. We are sleepwalking into the end of days.

China imposed its one-child-per-couple policy in an attempt to stem its population growth. This ran counter to its greater ambition to be the biggest and most powerful country in the world, reducing its future workforce and creating an ageing population. The Chinese government has now quietly abandoned the policy. Had they persisted with it, the population would have halved in thirty years, yet China would still have had a greater population than the US of A.

China recently planted six billion trees – mostly in its northern territories – in an attempt to reverse the desertification of those areas. Sounds like a lot; in fact, it's only two or three trees per person.

The limitations of a tree are that it is mute and immobile. It depends on its ability to cast spells on humans, releasing endorphins in our brain that make us love and protect it. I am among the spellbound. I am conscious of the trees guiding my pen, but I am sufficiently critical to recognise that a tree is self-serving. Its leaves are able to take carbon dioxide from the air and, through photosynthesis, separate the carbon from the oxygen. The leaf sends the carbon down its twig, along its branch and to its trunk to make the tree grow. We praise the trees for inhaling our deadly foe, CO_2, and gifting us their oxygen, but for the tree, oxygen is merely the waste material of the process. Nevertheless, it sustains us.

Despite my warnings, my son, Lee, has joined me as a tree slave.

> He climbed to the top of every tree,
> Conquered them one by one,

Raised a boyish arm in victory.
Now a man lured back by oaks,
He found the trees had conquered him,
And serves them all his days.

Up here in the Wicklow hills, we live among these oxygen-makers. In Dublin, vehicles, people and industry are all gulping oxygen, yet the percentage of oxygen in the air, both here and there, is always the same: 21 per cent. Beats me.

Dr Sam Synge, the brother of the playwright John Millington Synge, was the vicar here in the 1920s. He probably planted the exotic trees – which all seem to be around a hundred years old – as well as the English imports, like the chestnut.

The chestnut tree is the first to leaf,
And first to drop them in the fall.
In case it has not caught the eye,
It flaunts huge white flowers,
Like candles on a Christmas tree.
The glossy nut conceals a delicate flesh
that nobody eats any more.
Conkers is a forgotten game,
Nuts lay unwanted on grassy floor.
Finally recall what they are for,
And shoot roots down into the soil.

My only chestnut stands next to my only beech, like suspects in an identity parade. In Ireland, the Office of Public Works decided to cut down all the beech trees in public places because they are not indigenous, only naturalised, like me. However, there was such an outcry at the slaughter of this beautiful tree that the OPW was forced to recant.

The native oak built ships, bridges, cathedral roofs, furniture. My brother-in-law, a Cornish boat-builder, would select a growing oak that had branches bent at the right angles for his purpose: the making of a Mevagissey lugger.

I love the ancient oaks I inherited. They are at the top of a steep slope. They are primeval. They or their predecessors have always been there, since the time when northern Europe was covered in oak.

Oaks on Slopes

Old oaks are mostly found on slopes,
For on any land fit to grow or graze,
The oak was felled and fashioned into boats,
Or floorboards or to keep the fire ablaze.
Once the master of all the land
It now clings to slopes as best it can.

The beguiling mystery of the Great Oak is that it is rooted much further down the slope than the other oaks yet soars over them, and its rich fan of leaves goes high above them. I marvel at it every day and revere it. To set eyes on the Great Oak, remote in its lofty silence, is to be astonished that Nature could conjure up a creature of such huge, harmonious beauty; for Nature is wild and a turmoil of forces, storms and floods, earthquakes and wild fires and erupting volcanoes. When we occasionally encounter a perfect summer's day, we wish it would go on for ever, but after a few such days, we yearn for a flurry of snow or to hear the wind stirring the leaves.

Winds do not blow, they suck: air is sucked from high- to low-pressure areas, levelling the pressure and keeping the air breathable. We and Nature are in a flimsy compact to keep things going.

Steel has taken the strain from the oaks, and we tree slaves are busily replanting them. Welcome back to the flat lands, noble oaks.

My Great Oak leans over the river. I notice that it has recently dropped two large boughs onto the riverside, reducing a lot of the strain. Which part of the oak makes that calculation and then the decision to reduce the strain? Is it the intelligent fungi that tangle in the tree's roots? Or the cambium layer, where so many of the tree's functions are controlled?

A tree's acorns or seeds contain all the information about its shape and size. We take this for granted, but when you hold a tiny acorn up against the majesty of the Great Oak, you wonder at the microscopic intensity of the seed.

In 1897 it was fashionable to plant a monkey puzzle tree to celebrate Queen Victoria's Diamond Jubilee. They all began to die towards the end of the twentieth century, as they reached a hundred years of age. If ours was planted by Dr Synge in the 1920s, it must be approaching its demise, but happily shows no sign of it.

I expect Dr Synge was responsible for the cluster of lime trees as well.

Dr Sam Synge's son, John, was born in the house in which I now live. I got to know him when I arrived here fifty years ago. He told me that his father had been a medical missionary to China and took this living on his return. The rectory was probably in the gift of his brother, John Millington, who was lord of all he surveyed. He lived just down the hill, though his majestic house is now in ruins. His poetry is seldom read, but his play *The Playboy of the Western World* is a classic that is often revived. Dr Synge was a bee-keeper, said John, which would account for the lime trees, from which the bees produced incomparable honey, pellucid, with a dizzying aroma.

When I got here, half a century ago, I discovered a walled garden that had been so colonised by brambles that we needed machetes to get in. We eventually repaired the walls and planted an orchard and a vegetable garden.

According to the deeds, I seem to be the first individual to have owned these acres (though I prefer the term 'loaned', rather than 'owned'). Before they were taken by the Church of Ireland, they were part of the monastic lands of nearby Glendalough, the holiest place in Ireland. St Kevin lived in a cave on the edge of Glendalough lake, and rumours of his miracles attracted monks from far and wide. They built a monastery and no fewer than seven churches, some of which survive, though none are open for business. What drove the monks to abandon this place? Was it ravaged by the Vikings?

In my film *I Dreamt I Woke Up*, I suggested that an energetic force came from the lake that Kevin had harnessed for his own ends, as the Druids had done before him. If the force was not harnessed, it would run wild and cause all sorts of trouble. Today, the lake seems dead. Thousands of tourists come and stare at it. Perhaps they have stared it to death.

Like so many lapsed or no-longer-believing Christians, I have a nostalgia for the Church, for its spires reaching for the heavens, its pleading psalms, the music, from Bach to Mozart. Two thousand years is a long time to wait for the Second Coming.

I was sure I would die young, so I hurried to get my work done, and here I am at eighty-eight. Like a dying sycamore, I can't walk unaided, I'm hard of hearing, with fading eyesight, yet I'm still sending out a few leaves.

Twenty years ago, when my eldest daughter, Telsche, died so very young, we planted a Himalayan silver birch in her name. I wrote a poem about her that ended:

> I can peel off its silver parchment bark,
> And write upon it a loving letter,
> But to whom?

I have an answer: to her daughter, Daphne. She was seven when her mother died.

For Daphne

> My children now have children too,
> And the child of my eldest child
> Has two mighty sons herself.
> Thus the Race goes racing on,
> Obeying instincts on a raft of love,
> A love that swells with every birth,
> A love that holds us all aloft,
> Above the waves that crash below,
> On wings both strong and feather soft.

I was broken by the death of Daphne's mother, my daughter Telsche. I have never mended. I am patched up, as I am in this book, hung out here for all to see. Why do I write of Telsche? Because her life flickers to life when I write of it.

An arboretum like mine is a kind of zoo for trees, but many species of tree are planted and felled for commercial reasons. The humble spruce makes our newspapers, and many other species are used to make books, toilet rolls and glossy certificates of professional attainment. The endless monotony of the trees of Canada are harvested like wheat and pulped. Growing or felled or fashioned into furniture or made into books, the tree is all around us. Floorboards are grown as we walk on them. We are dependent upon wood, dead or alive.

For forty years Garech Browne and I were very devoted but ill-
matched friends.
He, the aristocrat; I, the commonest of commoners.
I am a republican who comes from a kingdom; he a royalist who
comes from a republic.
He was always late, and I am always on time and first on the set.
I was a workaholic, and he was an alcoholic.

Garech lived in his exquisite Gothic house, Luggala, looking out over his private lake, Lough Tay. The Avonmore River drains his lake and passes through my land, confirming our connection. Champagne was on offer at any hour, day or night, at

Luggala

Rain hammers granite rock,
Bounces into furious mist,
Races down the mountainside,
Roaring and white at Luggala,
Where Garech dispenses *noblesse oblige*
to pipers and poets all under siege.

Sublime music keeps the storm at bay,
The deluge swerves past the house,
A wall of water judders the sepulchre,
A brother and sister tremble below.
Lough Tay swallows the angry rain
Into its magical, glacial depths.
Merlin conjured Excalibur from here
To serve a telling of the myth.
Swollen, bursting Lough Tay
Disgorges the riotous water
Into a rocky stretch of river
That puts manners on it, slows it.
Turns up tamed at Loch Dan,
Gently cradled by soft hills,
Its shallow shingle sought by salmon
To lay their eggs and die all spent.
The Avonmore River drains it all,
Two lakes and a mountainside.
The weight of water runs for the sea,
But not before passing me.
I stand at my swimming hole
As the river hurtles past.
'Come with me,' the river calls,
'Come with me to the sea.'
A perfect way to go, but courage fails.

On summer days, I stand on its bank,
Naked, waiting to be invited in.
Unworthy, the river will not have me.
On days when I am granted entry,

I swim across to the rock of truth,
Embraced, washed clean of sin,
The wanted wordless benediction.

Poor, rich Garech
Would not be saved.
He found the death
So urgently craved.
Gone a little too soon,
Choked on his silver spoon.

I miss his innocent wisdom and his house and lake, but most of all his pessimism, which always cheered me up no end. He was an exasperating misfit, born into the wrong century, surviving on champagne and Luggala air.

As my friends die off, I am whittled down, and my own demise comes closer. In the tumult and stress and magic of making movies, all thoughts of death are banished, but for an old man, Death is a constant companion. He is always there, offering me a game of chess. I have partially defeated him by putting Lee Marvin up there in his pomp for ever, or for as long as the Library of Congress exists and protects *Point Blank*.

I do the crossword to check for memory loss, press-ups for the mind. My mother's memory let her down in her early nineties. 'I have the gift of forgetting,' she said. At eighty-eight, I am heading that way. Shoot me when mine goes.

The recognition that we need to revise our contract with Nature has brought about the notion of wilding. My guilt about neglecting two meadows is salved by discovering that I was doing the right thing all along.

Weeds

We have cut you and mowed you,
Uprooted and sprayed you,
Tried to eliminate you,
Kept our lawns free of you,
But underground warfare persisted.
Wilding has made us admit our mistakes,
Our crimes have been shamefully listed,
We regret our cruelty and hate,
Wilding has taught us to love instead.
Welcome back, dear Dandelion,
Come home, purple Thistle,
Feel safe, yellow Ragwort
Rejoice, golden gorse,
Whatever your colour or race,
You may now safely show your face.

An arboretum like mine is a zoo for trees. Wood is everywhere. I have a sturdy oak kitchen table at which friends and wives and children have eaten, wined, argued, laughed and shared our stories. How often we have thumped it to make a point, and it has never flinched or stirred. Now my wife Hope has shaved it and rubbed it with beeswax, and it glows deeply and darkly.

I was an autodidact, drunk on books. Books are made of trees. I have had more than my share of books and trees. I was sorting through my archive as I prepared to send it to the Lilly Library at the University of Indiana, when I was confronted by a huge pile of exercise books, journals I had kept from the age of sixteen until I started directing film at the BBC, for directing's demands exclude all else. I browsed through them: leaving school at sixteen, wanting to be a writer but not knowing how to go about it, bedsitter life, one-finger typing, on the knocker, dismal streets, dry-cleaning, stories published, BBC youth programmes take notice, I am on the air, haunting the hallowed halls, interviewing film crews, yearning to join this secret society, conscription intervenes, army life, learning to edit film, marriage, babies.

Lilly will put the archive online. Should I send the journals or destroy them? Writing them was a process of discovery; ideas sprung out of them. These journals were a conversation with my subconscious, except I did not know its name. Some of them are silly and immature. Finally, I decide to send them with the rest of my archive, where they will rest alongside those of Orson Welles and John Ford.

In a lifetime spent observing Nature, I have often marvelled at how a newborn swallow, for instance, can navigate its way to Africa alone. This is what Darwin describes as imprinted behaviour. Does imprinting mark the end of the evolution of species?

Recently, we have learnt that our subconscious makes decisions for us, guides us and supplies us with ideas. 'An idea came to me' – it came from the subconscious. Martin Amis has described how when he is in full flow, it is like taking dictation. We all know people, often very clever, who lack connection. There was one such at school. He was a much better chess player than me, but I nearly always beat him. 'Only connect.'

Is it possible that some form of the enabling subconscious

underpins all animal and plant life, telling trees when to leaf, flowers when to bloom? Is disease and death caused by a disconnect from that source?

If so, is old age a loosening of that connection?

Old Age

1 He had long since lost his grip on time.
The hours stretched out,
But the days raced by,
Years passed in the blink of an eye.
He used to be a boy so bold,
How did he get so very old?

2 Waking up at five in bed,
His room blackened by night,
'Am I alive or dead?' he cries.
But when he tried to arise,
Aches and pains and feeling sick
Confirmed he was still among the quick.

3 What a great relief it is
To be free of needing sex.
He doesn't care now how he looks,
Nor what the hell he wears,
Or even how badly he behaves,
For he's no longer 'passion's slave'.

4 He complained bitterly to her,
'I have searched everywhere

For my slippers lined with fur.
You know I keep them under my seat.'
'Well, try looking on your feet.'

5 Double vision is not all bad.
Two moons waning in the sky,
Two daughters dance in perfect step.
But if he wants to read a book,
He must close one eye
To look.

6 Sometimes words escape him.
If he patiently awaits,
They float up and rejoin him.
If that fails to salve his anguish,
He goes down to the cellar,
Where they mostly languish,
And drags them, damaged, back to life.
They stutter or mispronounce,
But carry meaning nonetheless.
The cellar is seeping water, he sees.
He fears that some words,
Will drown and be lost for ever.
For alas we cannot remember
Words we have forgotten.

7 Last night a tall birch tree fell,
A sapling he planted forty years ago
To nurse young oaks against the wind.
The old man searched for the fallen tree.

The wind that felled the tree felled him too.
They found him lying dead in a ditch,
His quest had by ten feet failed,
Prevailing wind had again prevailed.

8 I am on my very last lap,
I spy the finishing line.
My friends have all dropped out,
I cross the line alone.
No tape left for me to breach,
No crowd to urge me on.
I hear their distant voices,
As they cheer another race on.

Creed: I believe in the air I breathe, until I don't.

October 2021

INDEX